Marx's Litera

A poet, essayist, and philosopher in the Marxist tradition, **Ludovico Silva Michelena** (1937–88) was one of the most important Venezuelan intellectuals of the twentieth century. His books include *La plusvalía ideológica* (*Ideological Surplus-Value*) and *Anti-manual para uso de marxistas, marxólogos y marxianos* (*Anti-Handbook for Marxists, Marxologists, and Marxians*).

Marx's Literary Style

Ludovico Silva

Translated by Paco Brito Núñez

Foreword by Alberto Toscano

VERSO

London • New York

First published in English by Verso 2023
Translation © Paco Brito Núñez 2023
First published as *El estilo literario de Marx*
© Siglo XXI Editores 1975
Foreword © Alberto Toscano 2023

1 3 5 7 9 10 8 6 4 2

Verso
UK: 6 Meard Street, London W1F 0EG
US: 388 Atlantic Avenue, Brooklyn, NY 11217
versobooks.com

Verso is the imprint of New Left Books

ISBN-13: 978-1-83976-553-7
ISBN-13: 978-1-83976-554-4 (UK EBK)
ISBN-13: 978-1-83976-555-1 (US EBK)

British Library Cataloguing in Publication Data
A catalogue record for this book is available from the British Library

Library of Congress Cataloging-in-Publication Data
A catalog record for this book is available from the Library of Congress

Typeset in Minion by Biblichor Ltd, Scotland
Printed and bound by CPI Group (UK) Ltd, Croydon CR0 4YY

I dedicate this essay to my dear teacher Juan García Bacca: a great scholar of Marx, a great scholar of the relationship between science and style, and a great stylist in his own right. I am sure that in writing about Marx's style, he would have enjoyed starting out from the following words by Machado and Marx:

'Words, as opposed to stones, or colour-imparting substances, or moving air, are, in and of themselves, signifiers of the human, which the poet must imbue with new meanings. A word is, in part, an exchange-value, *a social product, a tool of objectivity (objectivity meaning, in this case, a convention between subjects), and the poet aims to make it into the means of expression of an individual psyche, a singular object, a* qualitative value. *The difference between a word spoken by everyone and a lyric word is the same as the difference between a coin and a piece of jewellery made from the same metal.'*

Antonio Machado

'Language is practical consciousness.'

Karl Marx

Contents

Foreword: Echoes of Marx

Sólo desde la tierra se puede ver el cielo
L. Silva, 'Carta materialista a mi madre' (1973)

Marking the 150th anniversary of *The Communist Manifesto* with an article on that text's style, the novelist and semiotician Umberto Eco prefaced his remarks by calling for the republishing of *Lo stile letterario di Marx*, the 1973 Italian translation of the book you hold in your hands.[1] While the question of Marx's style has not been ignored by his legions of commentators (and detractors), Eco's reminiscence testifies to the lack of concerted treatments of how Marx produced himself as an author. That said, Marx's style was not a marginal matter for his contemporaries. His comrade and disciple, Wilhelm Liebknecht, and his first biographer, Franz Mehring – socialist activists who were also academically trained philologists – both illuminated aspects of Marx's literary and critical artistry that Silva's volume explores with nuance and combativeness.

---

1   In a 1986 conference, 'El marxismo come aristocracia' (originally published in *La interpretación feminina de la historia y otros ensayos*, Centauro, 1987), Silva notes that, despite the healthy sales of *El estilo literario de Marx*, he never received any royalties from Italy, though he does mention the 'very generous critical reception of men like Umberto Cerroni, that great philosopher of the PCI who was daring enough to call me – a simple citizen of an underdeveloped country which no one knows except for its oil – nothing less than "a very intelligent man": something which, spoken in Europe, must be considered by us as disproportionate praise'. Now in *Ensayos escogidos*, El perro y la rana, 2014, p. 100.

In his *Biographical Memoirs* (1896), Liebknecht pushes back against claims that the author of *Capital* was plagued with a bad style or was altogether bereft of one. While castigating those philistine 'polishers of words and twisters of phrases who have not understood and were not capable of . . . following the flight of [Marx's] genius to the highest peaks of science and passion and into the lowest depths of human misery and human baseness', Liebknecht underscores that such pejorative judgements stem from the incapacity to see the signature of Marx's thought and person behind the surface heterogeneity of his products. The plethoric sarcasm of *Herr Vogt*, the dialectical complexity of *Capital*, the polemical bravura of the *Eighteenth Brumaire* – all corroborate the principle that the 'style is not only the man, it is also the subject-matter – and it must be adapted to the latter'. Liebknecht, editor of the Social Democratic Party newspapers *Der Volkstaat* and *Vorwärts*, is particularly attuned to the political violence of Marx's craft:

> Is the *Eighteenth Brumaire* unintelligible? Is the dart incomprehensible that flies straight at his target and pierces the flesh? Is the spear unintelligible that, hurled by a steady hand, penetrates the heart of the enemy? The words of the *Brumaire* are darts, are spears – they are a style that stigmatizes, kills. If hate, if scorn, if burning love of freedom ever found expression in flaming, annihilating, elevating words, then it is surely in the *Eighteenth Brumaire*, in which the aroused seriousness of Tacitus is united to the deadly satire of Juvenal and the holy wrath of Dante. The style is here what it – the stylus – originally was in the hands of the Romans – a sharp-pointed steel pencil for writing and for stabbing.[2]

A few years later, on occasion of the twenty-fifth anniversary of Marx's death, Mehring would remark that, while a comprehensive

---

2 Wilhelm Liebknecht, *Karl Marx: Biographical Memoirs*, trans. Ernest Untermann, Charles Kerr & Co., 1906, pp. 75–6.

inquiry into his style would make a signal contribution to the understanding of Marx's work, 'the task would be difficult, and it is not one of those immediately incumbent on his heirs' – busy as they were struggling over how best to actualize his political legacy. Yet Mehring did think it was imperative to provide some local resistance to bourgeois scientists' maligning of Marx's style and method, which came down to one question:

> From Herr Wilhelm Roscher down to the youngest university instructor, they all complain of his passion for metaphor. Marx's fondness for the use of figurative language is indisputable: but what these adversaries mean to convey by the accusation is that though his intelligence may have been brilliant, it was certainly not acute; that, entangled in 'obscure mysticism', he could only elucidate even the doctrine of historical materialism quite vaguely, and with the use of a 'patchwork of imagery'.[3]

Mehring countered this objection first by referring to Aristotle's view of genius as grounded in the capacity to recognize likeness (*to homoion theorein*), and then via a portable history of the theory of metaphor in German letters, beginning with Luther's Bible translation (formative for Marx), moving through the metaphorical inflation of movements like euphuism and Marinism, and culminating in the consolidation of a thinking and practice of metaphor in Lessing, Goethe and Hegel – a consummate metaphor-maker who bequeathed to Marx some of the literary and cognitive tools with which he would forge dialectical images of capital's metaphysical manifestation, like the section of *Capital* on commodity fetishism, which still proves so indecipherable to bourgeois economists. They, Mehring sardonically

---

3   Franz Mehring, 'Karl Marx and Metaphor', in *Karl Marx: Man, Thinker, and Revolutionist. A Symposium edited by D. Ryazanoff,* Martin Lawrence, 1927, p. 96. Marx spoofs Roscher's prose mercilessly in a footnote to *Capital, Volume 1.*

observes, counter Marx's use of metaphors with what they advertise as conceptual analysis, but which, on closer inspection, turns out to be 'an unending shadow-dance of metaphysical notions, which momentously glides along the walls of the capitalist prison-house', trying to hold at bay 'the racy metaphors of revolutionary dialectic'.[4]

The relation between concepts, categories and metaphors is among the salient concerns of Silva's study. That he was able to tackle the difficult task of elucidating Marx's style is also a function of the Venezuelan writer's biographical and intellectual trajectory, of what he termed the 'profound duality of my intellectual life, divided between the essayist and the poet'.[5] Born Luis José Silva Michelena in 1937 to a well-to-do family in Caracas (his older brothers José Agustin and Héctor were prominent academics, the first a sociologist and anthropologist, the second an economist whose contributions to dependency theory would influence his younger brother), after attending a private Jesuit college Ludovico continued his education in Europe between 1954 and 1960. There he studied philosophy and literature in Madrid (where fellow student-poets baptized him with the name he would use from then on), French literature at the Sorbonne and Romance philology at Freiburg under Hugo Friedrich, whose readings of Baudelaire, Rimbaud and Mallarmé in *The Structure of Modern Poetry* would hold an abiding influence over Silva – introducing him not just to formal study of *les poètes maudits* but to what he called the 'dense and jagged, if ultimately tender, forest of the German language'.[6]

---

4   Mehring, 'Karl Marx and Metaphor', p. 101. See also Mehring's comments on the difference and complementarity of Marx and Engels's styles in *Karl Marx: The Story of His Life*, trans. Edward Fitzgerald, University of Michigan Press, 1962, p. 232.

5   Ludovico Silva, 'Jorge Guillén el poeta de oro', in *Belleza y revolución*, new ed., Fundación para la Cultura y las Artes, 2019 [1979], p. 63.

6   Ludovico Silva, 'Hugo Friedrich', in *Belleza y revolución*, p. 122.

Upon returning to Venezuela, Silva began establishing himself as a poet and essayist – his first collection, *Tenebra*, is from 1964, while his second book, *Boom!!!* (1965), a poem on nuclear warfare in the wake of the Cuban Missile Crisis, would be prefaced by Thomas Merton.[7] For Silva, poetry was 'an indispensable weapon to attain a genuine knowledge of things. It is, in its deepest essence, dialectics.'[8] He was also intensely active on the cultural front, serving as the general secretary of the Ateneo de Caracas and founder of its journal *Papeles*, co-founding the journal *Lamigal*, and writing for the newspaper *El Clarín* and the literary journals *Sol Cuello Cortado, Cal* and *El Corno Emplumado*. While sympathetic to political and not just artistic vanguards, Silva seems to have kept a distance from the organizations of the revolutionary left and the guerrilla formations they bodied forth (though he was apparently sympathetic to the Movimiento de Izquierda Revolucionaria, abhorred the Venezuelan Communist Party, and in the 1970s would refer positively both to Yugoslav experiments with self-management and to the experience of *poder popular* in Matanzas, Cuba).[9] From 1970, he would teach philosophy at the Central University of Venezuela.

Silva's life seems to have borne greater affinities with Baudelaire's (or Bukowski's) than with that of a typical revolutionary militant or theorist. As his brother Héctor reminisced: 'Tormented existence? Yes! Together we traveled to alcohol's chiaroscuro kingdom, together we caroused in the bars and taverns in the whirlwind of the República del Este and the Callejón de la Puñalada, together we gave food and drink to beggars and gangsters at high dawn.'[10] In 1986, Silva would be briefly committed to

---

7   See Ludovico Silva, *Opera poética, 1958–1982*, Ediciones de la Presidencia de la República, 1988.

8   Silva, 'Jorge Guillén el poeta de oro', p. 67.

9   Silva, *Belleza y revolución*, pp. 21–2 and 331 (in a speech on the 'future memory of Che Guevara' entitled 'The Man of the Twenty-First Century').

10 Héctor Silva Michelena, 'Los huesos andantes de Ludovico', *Papel Literario, El Nacional*, 21 March 2009; English translation at

an asylum for the mental disturbances caused by 'a demonic acid they called ammonium', generated by his alcohol consumption – an experience recorded in short harrowing and delirious texts, scribbled on any available surface, including cigarette packets, and published posthumously as *Papeles desde el amonio*. He would die two years later, at the age of fifty-one, of a heart attack caused by cirrhosis of the liver.

It was only in the context of a global '68 that a relatively mature Silva would undertake his reading of Marx and very quickly become a prominent reference in Latin American debates. By his own account, he was impelled in this direction not just by political turbulence and a deep dissatisfaction with the Marxism of party hacks and their handbooks (which he would skewer in his 1975 *Anti-manual*),[11] but by the teaching of two Spanish-Venezuelan philosophers teaching at the Central University of Venezuela, where Silva would obtain his philosophy degree in 1972 – Federico Riu, a former student of Eugen Fink and of Heidegger, whose Caracas seminar on Sartre was a significant inspiration, and Juan David García Bacca, to whom this book is dedicated and whose work Silva would celebrate in his *Belleza y revolución*.

Beginning with two books released in 1970, *La plusvalía ideológica* and *Sobre el socialismo y los intelectuales*, Silva would go on to publish numerous books and essays on Marx and Marxism, centred on the interlocking problems of *ideology* and *alienation* as they impacted upon the critique of capitalism and the concrete utopia of socialism, grasped in the context of the development of underdevelopment and (cultural) imperialism in South America.[12]

---

venepoetics.blogspot.com. The República del Este was a parodic and oppositional cultural formation headed by the poet Caupolicán Ovalles.

11   Ludovico Silva, *Anti-manual para uso de marxistas, marxólogos y marxianos*, Monte Ávila, 1975.

12   See *Sobre el socialismo y los intelectuales*, Ediciones Bárbara, 1970; *La plusvalía ideológica*, UCV, 1970; *Marx y la alienación*, Monte Ávila, 1974; *La alienación en el joven Marx*, Nuestro Tiempo, 1979; *Teoría del socialismo*, Editorial Ateneo de Caracas, 1980; *Humanismo*

In dialogue with Marcuse, Löwenthal, Horkheimer and Adorno, but also his friend, the poet and essayist Hans Magnus Enzensberger, Silva developed the notion of *ideological surplus-value*. In an essay on television as the ideological medium par excellence, the commodity which lets us see all the other commodities – which some commentators regard as foundational to the critical study of communication in Latin America[13] – Silva articulates this novel notion to capture the production of subjectivity under conditions of dependency and imperialism, what he terms the 'interiorization of underdevelopment'. As he writes:

> The system of dependency operated shrewdly. Together with material estrangement [*enajenación*] it came to form a kind of ideological estrangement at the mental level: a great ideal reservoir of loyalties toward the system itself, an ideological capital always ready to betray any subversive impulse and ever at the service of material capital. Together with the material surplus-value extracted from labour-power, the system of dependency gradually formed a mechanism to produce *ideological surplus-value*, through which the non-conscious part of people's psychic energy comes to form part of imperialist ideological capital, sustaining it, preserving it, perpetuating it.[14]

clásico y humanismo marxista, Monte Ávila, 1982; *La alienación como sistema: Teoría de la alienación en la obra de Marx*, Alfadil Ediciones, 1983. Silva would also be the object of a book-length criticism: Rafael Ramírez, *La intelectualidad impotente. Crítica de la obra de Ludovico Silva*, Universidad Central de Venezuela, 1981; see also Humberto Zavala, 'Apuntes críticos al concepto "ideología" en Ludovico Silva', *La Izquierda Diario*, supplement, 27 September 2020, at laizquierdadiario.com.ve.

13   See for example Jorge Alberto Calles-Santillana, 'Ludovico Silva and the Move to Critical Stances in Latin American Communication Studies', *Javnost – The Public*, Vol. 13, No. 3 (2006), pp. 69–80.

14   Ludovico Silva, 'El sueño insomne. Ideas sobre television, subdesarrollo, ideología', in *Teoría y práctica de la ideología*, Editorial Nuestro Tiempo, 1971, p. 164.

We might say that, where the ideological surplus largely operates behind our backs, style, as manifest in the person and writing of Marx, is a matter of the political appropriation of our unconscious as social individuals, the forging of a combative singularity open to the vast reservoirs of world literature and the world's languages – as well as, and above all, to the collective historical sedimentations and idiosyncrasies of one's idiom.[15] This understanding of style is also open to its bodily basis, as in the observation that the *Grundrisse* is a difficult text 'because its literary style reflects the deadly tiredness of that man who, in London, spent his days working as a journalist just to live badly, while he was up nights until four in the morning, between innumerable cigarettes and an empty stomach', labouring on his critique of political economy.[16]

In Silva's discussion of irony and alienation in this book's epilogue, he enjoins us not to follow in the tracks of so much Marxist scholasticism, which mistreats Marx's style as something that could be regarded as surplus to his science. Marx's personal, polemical, and literary temperament cannot be hived off from the temperament of his theory – irony, mockery, and

---

15   For a compelling account of and contribution to the Marxist study of style, see Daniel Hartley, *The Politics of Style: Towards a Marxist Poetics*, Brill, 2017. The reading of Silva's essay should be complemented by S.S. Prawer's magisterial study of Marx's uses of literature, *Karl Marx and World Literature* (Oxford University Press, 1976), which is especially enlightening on Marx as a critic of the (politics of) style of other writers. In *The German Ideology*, for instance, 'metaphors, grammatical constructions, even prose-rhythms are examined in an effort to demonstrate an opponent's incompetence, illogicality, or lack of imagination' (p. 122) – a tactic that Marx would also undertake in texts like 'Revelations about the Trial of Communists at Cologne' (1853) or the 1875 *Critique of the Gotha Programme*. As Prawer notes, Marx 'found in some of the techniques of literary criticism – metrical and rhythmic analysis, scrutiny of imagery, scrutiny of sentence-structures – a powerful means of discrediting his opponents' opinions along with their style' (p. 417).

16   Ludovico Silva, *En busca del socialismo perdido*, Fundación para la Cultura y las Artes, 2017, p. 127.

critique (including of the ad hominem variety) are *constitutive* of his social theory. 'To be able to imitate Marx's style gracefully,' Silva warns, 'one would need to recall that the entire machinery of his indignation is mounted on the serrated gear of his irony.' Silva's contention that the expression of the dialectic and the dialectic of expression are inseparable, that critique cannot be separated from style, finds its emblem and evidence in a phrase from *Class Struggles in France* where the theory of ideology and alienation finds full incarnation in syntax. Silva would return to it close to the end of his life, while advancing the scandalous if cogent proposition that Marx was an aristocratic thinker. Riffing off Stendhal's comments on Napoleon's Civil Code as a paragon of economy and efficacy in expression, Silva writes of how Marx

> was able to create a style and a way of thinking and writing endowed with the loftiest virtues of the aristocracy, namely, the musical elegance of phrases, his dialectical manner of beginning a sentence abruptly to then make an about-turn and go back to its starting point (this is the secret of the popularity enjoyed by many of Marx's phrases); his never-vulgar aggressiveness, his refined irony set like a diamond on the serrated wheel of his sentences, his way of saying things like: 'The mortgage the peasant has on heavenly possessions guarantees the mortgage the bourgeois has on peasant possessions', where the apodosis of the first prosodic syntagm makes a felicitous pirouette to land suddenly on the protasis; lastly, the grace and devastating precision that lends his science the appearance of a score by Cimarosa or Pergolesi, because of what Andrés Bello called 'smoothness' (*suavidad*), but which harbours in its interior an intellectual storminess worthy of Beethoven – all of this makes of his literary style a perfect demonstration of intellectual aristocracy.[17]

---

17   Silva, 'El marxismo come aristocracia', p. 102.

In this book, Silva will identify and explore three elementary aspects of Marx's style. First, an 'architectonic' perspective in which the scientific system and the aspiration to the work of art are inseparable – in keeping with Marx's own efforts to make conceptual dynamics plastic, perceptible. This is, of course, as any reader of Marx's masterpiece can testify, a very complex seeing and a very complex unity. Drawing on his own way with metaphors, Silva will speak of how, 'in *Capital*, categories are slowly embodied, bit by bit, as though we were dealing with a growing, ascending vegetation, which comes to blanket an ocean of abstractions'.[18] Second, he identifies a dialectic of expression that doubles as an expression of the dialectic, such that the 'formal and logical relations into which Marx places verbal *signs* constitute a plastic gesture aimed at reflecting the material and historical relations of *signifieds*'. Third, and crucially, there is Marx's unparalleled mastery of metaphors as cognitive and poetic instruments.

The pages devoted to the metaphors of superstructure, reflection and religion double as sharp polemics aimed at countless commentators who, insensitive to the internal economy of Marx's prose, would misunderstand them as theories in themselves, thereby failing truly to grasp the most monstrous and most spectral metaphor of all, capitalism. Many Marxists, impervious to the logic of Marx's style, have missed the style of his logic, while in trying to force metaphors into concepts they have ignored the lesson of Ortega y Gasset, for whom 'metaphor is an indispensable mental instrument, a form of scientific thought'.[19] As Silva would write in one of his several posthumously published works, in the twentieth century 'certain "Marxist" sectors have turned Marx's scientific categories (for example, alienation) into mere metaphors, but also the reverse: many of Marx and Engels'

---

18   Silva, 'Sobre el metodo en Marx', in *Anti-manual*, p. 184.
19   José Ortega y Gasset, 'Las dos grandes metáforas', in *El espectador* (1924), quoted by Silva in 'Escribir y filosofar', in *Belleza y revolución*, p. 300.

metaphors, such as the famous "superstructure" and "reflection", have been forcibly converted into scientific categories'.[20] A symptom of this methodological malady is discerned by Silva in the way the Marxist vulgate has retained only one of the two terms from that (un)fortunate expression in *The German Ideology*, *ideologische Reflexe und Echos*. As it is a dogmatic counterfactual, we are induced to wonder what kind of fierce debates and doctrinal revisions might have been generated if a 'theory of the echo' had arisen where we now puzzle over the 'theory of reflection'.[21]

If metaphor is a *translatio*, a transposition – not just from one meaning to another, but from one being to another[22] – then what Silva tried to diagnose and counter was a certain tendency to neglect the constitutive role of style in Marx, and thereby to generate pseudo-concepts (base and superstructure, reflection) as, so to speak, metaphors of metaphors, illegitimate and misleading transpositions of transpositions. And, while he often avowed, with self-deprecating irony, that he was not a Marxist in the sense of someone able to make the leap from interpretation

---

20   Ludovico Silva, *El combate por el nuevo mundo. Cultura, contracultura y alienación en Latinoamérica*, ed. Gabriel Jiménez Emán, Fábula Ediciones, 2017, p. 98. These posthumous publications – which include a *Teoría poética* (Editorial de la Universidad Simon Bolivar, 2008) – and reprints of earlier works have taken place in the context of the Bolivarian process in Venezuela, which has seen Silva celebrated and studied as a Marxist thinker in tune with the vision of 'twenty-first-century socialism'. The Escuela de Formación Política y Asuntos Amazónicos 'Ludovico Silva' was launched in 2011, while there are several Ludovico Silva–named chairs in Venezuelan universities.

21   Maybe this phase-shift from the visual to the sonic, the mirror and the panorama to the *acousmêtre* – those ideological echoes heard but unseen – is not just a sign of the pernicious effects of taking metaphors for concepts, but a theoretical possibility in its own right. That at least is what one could draw from the tonal critique of totality advanced by Fred Moten's dialogue with Fredric Jameson in *In the Break: The Aesthetics of the Black Radical Tradition*, University of Minnesota Press, 2003, pp. 211–31.

22   Silva, 'Escribir y filosofar', p. 300. See also the Epilogue in *Marx's Literary Style*.

to transformation, he did see his readings of Marx, this book very much included, as a contribution to a Marxism as heterodox, critical, irreverent and committed to the abolition of the world of capital as Marx himself was. In a short text entitled 'And Marxism?', he declared:

> Yes indeed, there are Marxists, including in Venezuela. It is not necessary that they all be in perfect agreement; even Marx did not agree with himself, which is why he said that he was not 'Marxist'. But Marxists are few, since not everybody is willing to take up an intellectual position that practically represents a war against everything that exists. Nor is it a matter of asking Marxist politicians that they adopt this stance in their tactics, even though we should when it comes to outlining a long-term strategy. Some time ago, we used to speak here of the 'long war'. The thesis, beyond bullets and rifles, remains in force. And so does the long war that a Marxist must wage against himself, which begins by reading Marx and never ends.[23]

Alberto Toscano
2022

---

23   Silva, '¿Y el marxismo?', in *Belleza y revolución*, p. 312.

Introduction

It is not difficult to guess the reaction the title of this essay will elicit in the reader. Marx's literary style? Was Marx even a literary figure? Is this, perhaps, a new study of Marx's ideas about art and literature?

Set these questions aside. Let us think about that phrase again: *Marx's literary style*. Marx was a writer; he left an imposing body of work. This work constitutes a scientific *corpus*, a theoretical text. But, along with a conceptual skeleton, this corpus possesses an expressive musculature: this theoretical text has been woven out of concrete literary threads. Its scientific system is supported by an expressive system.

In Marx, this system includes, or simply is, a literary style. It is *literary* because, just as, in practice, poetry encompasses a realm that goes beyond the bounds of verse and stretches to include many types of language, so too literature, as concept and practice, goes far beyond works of fiction and imagination and extends across the whole wide field of the written word. On top of that, Marx's expressive system constitutes a *style* – a peculiar, singular expressive genius that possesses certain characteristic verbal modes, certain analogical and metaphorical constants, its own vocabulary, its own economy and prosodic dance.

The concept of style is more restrictive than that of literature. All scientific writers, for instance, practise and possess a form of literary expression, but very few of them practise and possess a *style*. By style, I mean a genius consciously put in the service of a will to expression that is not content with the clean conscience that comes from having used the scientifically correct terms, but that also employs a literary conscience bent on making what is correct expressive and harmonious, a conscience that is ready to use every linguistic resource at its disposal to ensure that the logical construction of science is, at the same time, that science's architecture. Science loses nothing – in fact, it gains a lot – when it adds an illustrative rigour to its demonstrative rigour; nothing contributes to the comprehensibility of a theory like an appropriate metaphor or a fitting analogy.

In the case of Marx, his will-to-style carried him far. The part of his work that he was able to polish and publish constitutes, as he himself observed, 'an *artistic* whole', not only because of the architectonic quality it exhibits, but also because even its most insignificant details appear burnished, tensed and illuminated by a metaphorical art so consummate that one could say many of its concepts appear as *percepts*. In one of his youthful verses, Marx says of the poet:

Was er sinnet, erkennt, und was er fühlet, ersinnt.

He perceives what he thinks, and thinks what he feels.[1] This formula applies to the totality of Marx's oeuvre, and especially to texts such as the *Contribution to the Critique of Political Economy* (1859) or the first volume of *Capital* (1867), both of which, it bears saying, had the good fortune that eluded texts like the *Grundrisse*: they received the final pass – the incisive and minute finishing touch of a writer proud of his ability to form his phrases *artistically*, thereby giving his ideas an infinite plasticity which not only afforded them a greater accessibility but was also meant to confound, in practice, that species of verbal fetishism that makes scientific language a hieratic, abstruse, dead jargon

---

1   Karl Marx, 'On Hegel', in *Karl Marx and Friedrich Engels Collected Works*, Vol. 1, Lawrence and Wishart, 2010, p. 576. In this translation the line is rendered as: 'The Poet . . . understands what he thinks, freely invents what he feels.'

incapable of acting directly on the wider public. Thanks to this, any moderately educated person of the present day could read and enjoy that masterpiece of scientific prose, the *Contribution to the Critique of Political Economy*, taking in its content while simultaneously learning *to reason economically*. This is because all great thinkers who are also great stylists tend to present their work not as the result of previous thought but *as the process or act of thinking itself*: their readers are always present at the creation of their thinking, and they benefit from it because, instead of being forced to digest hardened thoughts, they are prompted to think, to rethink and to recreate the very act of theoretical discovery. Someone wholly ignorant of economics reading the *Critique* with the proper attention would be obligated to reason economically and rethink the entire edifice of the economy from its most primitive and abstract foundations, from its very stem cells: the commodity and value.

It looks as if Marx had decided to demonstrate, expressly through the practice of his style, that 'ideas' are not intangible or invisible but rather things that can be seen and perceived. Deeply knowledgeable of ancient Greek, he was aware that the word *idea* originally meant *external aspect, appearance* or *form*. When Plato in the *Protagoras* (315e) says τὴν ἰδέαν καλός, he simply means something like 'beautiful to look at' or 'beautiful in form'. The verb ἰδέαν meant nothing more than 'to see with one's own eyes'. And what did the word theory (θεωρία) signify if not the act of seeing, contemplating, observing?

In this way, Marx's thinking is something that can be plastically *perceived* – in his work, the conceptual has a perceptual value. His literary style is capable of granting the most complicated of abstractions the appearance of real *ideas* that possess colour and a graceful form. One can visualize his theories, and his conception of society can be metaphorically viewed as a gigantic architecture with an economic foundation or *Struktur* and an ideological superstructure or façade, its *Überbau*. His metaphors help us to *perceive* the properly scientific or theoretical content.

On another point, it is worth insisting on the necessity of not taking as explanations what are no more than metaphors or, inversely, mistaking explanations for metaphors. That inversion is common, and it leads to nothing less than a misunderstanding and falsification of Marx's thought and style. Against these misreadings – see the first and third sections of Chapter 2 – I propose a *stylistic* reading of Marx that is significant not only because it examines an unexplored dimension of Marx's thought but also, more importantly, because such a reading is indispensable for the proper discrimination between metaphors and theoretical explanations. These two aspects are so frequently conflated nowadays that there is hardly a Marxist who does not speak seriously of 'reflection theory' or of 'the theory of superstructure', despite the fact that such theories are not theories but metaphors. If Marx's work did not offer the most exhaustive scientific explanations along with these metaphors, then perhaps there would be a reason to confuse the two.

Marx's metaphors have led to such monumental and deep-seated confusion that it has become very difficult to set things straight. While his theories and ideas have become mere *beliefs* for many today, inversely, his principal metaphors have been taken for explanations. Absurd as this misrecognition is, 'faith' in Marx today is capable of swallowing anything, no matter how indigestible. It is all rather similar to something that Unamuno discussed, in his 1896 essay 'On the Reform of Spelling', concerning that famous line from the gospel: 'It is more difficult for a rich man to enter the Kingdom of Heaven than for a *camel* to pass through the eye of a needle.' Even in the classical era, the Greek *eta* (η) was read the same as the *iota* (ι) so that κάμηλον (*kamēlon*, camel) was read the same as κάμιλον (*kamilon*, cable or, according to Unamuno, cable-rope). Due to this confusion, there arose a spelling mistake whereby what ought to have been a 'cable' appeared as a 'camel', which makes a mess of the analogy. Even though this error was acknowledged for centuries, a huge number of ingenious explanations for the camel have arisen.

The same has happened with Marx's metaphors. When his work is treated *as gospel*, we are meant to accept camel for cable – 'superstructure' and 'reflection' are justified and accommodated as *explanations* of ideological phenomena. What the neo-evangelical commentators fail to see is that if ideology really were a superstructure or a reflection, then Marx would be, on the one hand, the most fervidly Platonist believer in a world of ideas apart from social structures, and, on the other, a defender of the absurd thesis that ideas and social values are nothing more than weak and passive reflections, aspects of an inactive mirror world.

In mentioning Unamuno, I am reminded of a stupendous word of his that suits Marx perfectly: *ideoclast*. If the iconoclasts break idols, then, Unamuno says of himself, I am an ideoclast who breaks ideas. And he says it in an article about *ideocracy*, the empire of ideas. Marx was a lifelong ideoclast, one of the fiercest and most fervent idea breakers of all time. This is one of the aspects of his literary and intellectual style which I will study here. Unamuno also said that his fight was against the *ideolog-ickers*. This is why few things are more similar than his literary style and Marx's. When it comes to implacably stigmatizing ideas and personages while preserving a serenity of reasoning, it is hard to find their equals. This is one of the most striking features of Marx's style – if perhaps not the most profound. It formed part of his *transformational* will, which went beyond pure and passive phenomenologies. This was brought to my attention by David García Bacca, himself a formidable stylist: 'Are we as philosophers so unfortunate that we can't go beyond our role of *phenomenologists* who describe what's immediately given and transubstantiate into *transformers* of immediate reality for the sake of what is profound and causal?'[2]

All of the features of Marx's style that this study takes up can be collected in and expressed by a contemporary linguistic

---

2 David García Bacca, *Humanismo teórico, práctico y positivo según Marx*, Fondo de Cultura Económica, 1965, p. 23.

category that, by a great coincidence, happens to go by the same name as Marx's main preoccupation: *economy*. The principle of economy in linguistics has been introduced by André Martinet. According to this principle, which is the principle of least effort, 'man does not expend his energies beyond what is needed to accomplish the goals he has set for himself'. Linguistic evolution is governed by the permanent antinomy between man's communicative needs and his tendency to reduce to a minimum his mental and physical activity. 'What can be called', Martinet writes, 'the economy of a language is this perpetual search for an equilibrium between communicative needs on the one hand and the inertias of memory and articulation on the other (keeping in mind that these last two are in permanent conflict). The play of all these factors is limited by a range of taboos that tend to freeze language by precluding any innovation that is too evident.' From this we can deduce that '*economy* is the appropriate frame to adopt when we seek to understand the *dynamics of language*'. Martinet explains that all languages are the economic products of the conflict between the unlimited needs of communication and the limited physical and mental resources of man.[3]

The point, then, is to understand that every language is *a system of forces in equilibrium*, a web of tensions (let us set aside, for now, the question of which economic theory is implicated here and whether it is an 'equilibrium theory' or not), and that this constitutes its dynamic, its movement. It is evident that style essentially consists of how a writer resolves the problem of linguistic economy. It is not, as Martinet tells us, about 'economizing' in the everyday sense of 'saving money', though sometimes a principle of saving is in play, as in the style of Azorín or that of the Frenchman Albert Camus. It is about *expending the appropriate amount of energy* on each page, neither more nor less. To use Martinet's example, *redundancy* is a

---

3 See also André Martinet, *Éléments de la linguistique générale*, Paris, 1960, chapter. 6, II, as well as the article on 'Economy' in *Linguistique: Guide alphabétique*, ed. André Martinet, Denöel, 1969, pp. 81ff.

linguistic phenomenon that is usually – contrary to popular belief – not about linguistic-economic 'waste' but, on the contrary, about an additional expenditure of energy that is necessary for effective communication. In verb conjugations ('soy'), there is an indication of the subject ('yo'), which means that it is redundant to say 'yo soy'; nevertheless, one does not communicate the same way with 'soy' as with 'yo soy'.[4] The additional expenditure has an expressive sense. In other cases, of course, redundancy does mean waste, as in Antonio Machado's example: the substitution of 'customary events that transpire in the thoroughfare' for 'what happens in the street'.

In the case of Marx, we have a literary style that makes constant use of this principle of linguistic economy. His metaphors constitute an additional expenditure of verbal energy that ensures *effective communication* with the reader. Many scientific writers consider additional expenditures of this kind inappropriate and silly; they do not seem to aspire to communication – in fact, some take an unhealthy pleasure in not being understood. For Marx, for whom *praxis* was the ultimate criterion of knowledge, it was indispensable to communicate practically with his public and to be understood so profoundly that he could influence the task of *Veränderung* – the subversive transformation of the world. That is why he took such care with his expressive economy. This is especially clear in the works he completed and published. In them, even the most insignificant figures and examples acquire a definite meaning. When he tells us that exchange-value makes all commodities the same, the example he gives us is as follows: 'one volume of Propertius and eight ounces of snuff may have the same exchange-value, despite the dissimilar use-values of snuff and elegies'.[5] Reaching for Propertius's

---

4   [*Trans.*: In Spanish, it is perfectly common and grammatically correct to leave out the pronoun 'yo' ('I') and simply say 'soy' to indicate 'yo soy' ('I am').]

5   Karl Marx, 'A Contribution to the Critique of Political Economy', in *Karl Marx and Friedrich Engels Collected Works*, Vol. 29, p. 270.

elegies might seem unnecessary, but it is a display of linguistic economy designed to help the reader understand the *universal alienation* (*allseitige Entäusserung*) of the use-values of all things that money brings about. In order to tell us about commodity fetishism, Marx uses formulas that would horrify any 'serious' economist, as when he claims that in the bourgeois world commodities appear as 'physically metaphysical' (*sinnlich übersinnlich*) things. But this is the economy of expression at its purest – a blow against all linguistic austerity or miserliness. Marx knew how to be concise and sober when he needed to be, but he also knew how to raise his voice, as in *The Communist Manifesto*, whose apocalyptic and poetic style serves a precise political purpose.

This principle of economy also operates in the *dynamics* of Marx's language. As we shall demonstrate in this essay (in the second section of Chapter 2, in particular), Marx constructed his phrases with the conscious intention of establishing a certain equilibrium of verbal forces meant to reproduce or express certain real antagonisms. In other words, he adapted his signs to his referents as carefully as he could. If there is anywhere that Marx's dialectics become manifest, it is in this linguistic play he engages in so often: he affirms something in a certain number of words, negates it in the same number of words but with an inverted syntactical order, and then synthesizes everything in a final phrase. Readers of this essay will find examples of the diverse stylistic variations on this move in Marx's work. It is one of the secrets of the 'roundedness' of many of his sentences, which has unfortunately caused them to circulate from hand to hand and to wear down like coins that have lost their original lustre. This is something that Marx himself, of course, would not have objected to, seeing as his ultimate goal was to bring about his own negation as an 'intellectual' and to have his work be reabsorbed by the people for whom it was written.

The principle of economy states: 'Man does not expend more force than is necessary to reach the goals he has set for himself.' This is the principle as viewed by a linguist. Now, Marx tells us in a famous passage in which he defines his global conception of society: 'Mankind . . . inevitably sets itself only such tasks as it is able to solve.'[6] Is it any wonder, then, that Marx would think of human society as fundamentally *economic*? 'No social order is ever destroyed before all the productive forces for which it is sufficient have been developed.'[7] The same happens in language: no language expires, barring a violent death, until it has developed all of its expressive possibilities.

But, even if this is the case at the social and historical level, it is not always true at the individual level. Just as every individual must strive to make history without waiting to be led or moved by some historical fate, every writer must strive to exhaust his expressive potential – his economico-linguistic communicative potential – without waiting for some destiny to make him understood. This is the only possible solution to the eternal theoretical conflict between historical necessity and individual freedom. This conflict does not exist at the level of the individual writer: anyone who does not exercise their maximum creative freedom in language cannot wait for historical necessity to make them into a great writer, just as history does not make those who turn their back on it great.

If what is called for today is to go beyond Marx by realizing him, instead of freezing him into taboos by wearing out his phrases through repetition, then this is because he developed his productive, creative capacities to their fullest extent, developed his expressive economy as far as it could go.

Caracas, April 1971

---

6   Karl Marx, 'Preface (to *A Contribution to the Critique of Political Economy*)', in *Early Writings*, trans. Rodney Livingstone and Gregory Benton, Penguin, 1992, p. 426.

7   Ibid., p. 426.

1

Marx's Literary Origins

Marx was not always a social scientist. He only became one around 1843–4 – a time when Lassalle's characterization of him as 'Hegel turned economist' (in a letter addressed to Marx on 12 May 1851) would have suited him well. Before that, he was a writer on politics and philosophy. And, earlier still, he had been a poet. Like many social scientists, Marx began as a literary intellectual.

These origins become important when we examine the fundamental features of his mature scientific work, that is, when we study the letter of his scientific spirit, his peculiar form of expressing the most complicated of economic problems with a lively formal splendour.

Auguste Cornu has narrated this first period of the young Marx's career in minute detail and with great care.[1] During this time, Marx assured his father that he had a definite literary and poetic vocation, and wrote delirious poetry while dedicating himself to all manner of aesthetic and mythological investigations.

But he was wrong, as he later realized: his vocation was not for *literature* itself, but for being a *writer*. His father helped him to see this when, with great benevolence and great precision, he suggested that his son's calling was not exactly that of a poet.

---

1 Auguste Cornu, *Karl Marx et Friedrich Engels: Leur vie et leur oeuvre*, tome I: *Les années d'enfance et de jeunesse, la gauche hégélienne, 1818/1820–1844*, Presses universitaires de France, 1955.

This is what Heinrich Marx wrote to Karl early in 1836: 'I tell you frankly, I am profoundly pleased at your aptitudes and I expect much from them, but it would grieve me to see you make your appearance as an ordinary poetaster.'[2]

Heinrich Marx was a very learned man, a great reader of Voltaire, Rousseau and Lessing, and he wielded considerable influence over his son. This was not the case with his mother, Henriette, whom Cornu describes as possessing a 'strictly practical' sense. How could a mother who, at the end of her days, derided her son for writing *Capital* instead of accruing capital have truly influenced this particular son?

Another influence on Marx – and on his literary taste in particular – was his father-in-law, Baron von Westphalen. Marx would eventually dedicate his doctoral thesis on the natural philosophy of Epicurus and Democritus to him. The baron could read Latin and Greek fluently, and certainly helped cultivate in Marx an unflagging love for the Greek language that he would use as a tool in crafting ironies aimed at bourgeois economists who would – as Marx tells Engels in a letter written while he was working on *Capital* – undoubtedly be scandalized by a treatise on economics that quoted Shakespeare and Homer (Marx's favourite poets), the latter – in an added insult – in the original Greek. They would take this as an offence against their economic *esprit de sérieux* and would see it as another reason to tar Marx's work as 'metaphysical', 'literary' and 'ideological' – epithets (the last in particular) still hurled today by a certain class of scientistic sociologist. That said, the lie wrapped up in these qualifiers does reveal – as all lies do – a certain truth: the author of *Capital* was a truly extravagant economist, who could move with equal assurance in the realms of the most taxing and concrete empirical details and of the most complex and subtle abstractions. An example of the first is the magisterial chapter on machinery and large-scale industry, which

---

2   'Heinrich Marx to Karl Marx', in *Karl Marx and Friedrich Engels Collected Works*, Vol. 1, p. 651.

contains – it is worth noting – a most detailed description of a clock's inner workings and in which diverse machines are taken apart, piece by piece. An example of his capacity for abstraction is the first chapter on the commodity, the very literary model of a synchronic analysis. From another angle, the extravagant side of Marx that has always irritated bourgeois scientists involves his combination of scientific objectivity with an indignant and combative denunciation of the social contradictions and hidden interests of political economy. Finally, it is astonishing that Marx could embody, in his own scientific person, something that he considered a basic condition of the move beyond alienation: *the overcoming of the division of labour.* He was neither a pure economist nor a pure sociologist, philosopher, literary intellectual or politician: he was a complete social scientist who would not have fitted into any of the modern university's 'specialized departments', just as he did not fit in at the German universities of his age, which he considered full of 'petulant and grumpy' academics who took themselves to be – the note of dialectical irony is unmissable – 'scourges of the bourgeoisie'.[3]

Let us return to his formative years. At seventeen, he writes a set of 'Reflections of a Young Man upon Choosing a Profession' in which he expresses, among other things, his sense that 'we cannot always attain the position to which we believe we are called; our relations in society have to some extent already begun to be established before we are in a position to determine them'.[4] This turned out to be a great truth for Marx himself: not only did he fail at what he considered his vocation – literature – he also abandoned the profession – jurisprudence – that his father had selected for him. Before he could determine his calling

---

3   Karl Marx, *Das Kapital*, 'Nachwort zur zweiten Auflage', in *Marx-Engels Werke*, Vol. 23, Dietz Verlag, 1962, p. 27.
4   Karl Marx, 'Reflections of a Young Man upon Choosing a Profession', in *Karl Marx and Friedrich Engels Collected Works*, Vol. 1, p. 4; cf. Franz Mehring, *Karl Marx: The Story of His Life*, p. 5.

himself, the student milieu he inhabited worked a slow and subtle influence that set his true vocation: a kind of social science that still operated under the signs of politics and philosophy. In his 'Reflections' he had also written: 'Those professions which are not so much involved in life itself as concerned with abstract truths are the most dangerous for the young man whose principles are not yet firm and whose convictions are not yet strong and unshakeable.'[5] Therein lies a first announcement of his future struggle against ideology.

In October 1835, Marx sails the Mosel on his way to Koblenz. From there, he takes a steamer to Bonn, where he arrives on the seventeenth. He matriculates at the university the same day. He had received instructions from his father underlining the convenience of studying law, as well as physics and chemistry (which is a bit strange). Marx wanted to sign up for nine courses, but his father convinced him to take just six in order to avoid a *surmenage* (there is no reason Heinrich Marx would have known that his son Karl was, as he himself would say years later, 'a machine for devouring books', or that, as Ruge would put it in a letter to Feuerbach on 15 May 1844, Marx's reading was 'a bottomless ocean'). Note the composition of the courses Marx selected:

- Puggé, *Encyclopaedia of the Law*
- Böcking, *Institutions*
- Walter, *History of Roman Law*
- Welcker, *Mythology of the Greeks and Romans*
- Schlegel, *Topics on Homer*
- D'Alton, *History of Modern Art*[6]

Only three courses on the law, and not even a hint of physics or chemistry. Instead, three courses on art and literature! None of

---

5   Marx, 'Reflections of a Young Man', p. 8.
6   Cornu, *Karl Marx et Friedrich Engels: Leur vie et leur oeuvre*, tome I, p. 69, note 2.

these selections would prove useless to Marx. When, along with Engels, he criticized the legal ideology of society, or when he developed his position on alienation and the state, he worked with concrete concepts he had learned in his youth. His mature penchant for drawing on ancient literature for his metaphors, his investigation (in the *Grundrisse*) of mythology as an expression of man's domination of nature, and, in short, the brilliance of his style, all speak to a thorough and deep-seated classical education.

This education is important for our subject. There is, at present, a tendency to deprecate the much-vaunted 'classical education'. There is an objective reason for this: for centuries, 'classical education' has served as the metropolitan tip of the spear of a 'Western culture' which has used beautiful filigrees to hide monstrosities such as racism, colonialism and imperialism. That culture was the clever and brilliant invention of capitalism. Clever, because the rise of worldwide commerce and the universalization of economic relations in the guise of trade occurred along with the development of a universal culture and a set of universal ideological 'values': capitalism was born thinking of itself as eternal and thinks of itself that way more than ever; in order to sustain this sense of self, it needed a culture that, despite being historical and concrete – it is, after all, just a small fraction of world history – conceives of itself and announces itself as eternal, as Culture par excellence. Brilliant, because it has produced brilliant works. Material slavery did not prevent imaginative beauty from arising in its very bosom.

Nevertheless, 'classical education' has its positive aspects, as all human formations do. There is nothing inherently wrong with the study of classical languages and ancient literature. To condemn these because they tend to be accompanied by a particular ideology is to confuse matters. It is perfectly plausible to imagine people devoting themselves to these studies in a socialist society. To suppress them – as there is a tendency to do – is to fall into the most unfortunate quid pro quo.

In Marx, for example, classical education produced excellent results, especially when it comes to his literary style. How does such an education influence the style of a writer? This is a difficult, but not impossible, question. Whoever seeks to answer it must draw on their own experience.

Everyone who has studied a dead language extensively – the way Marx studied Greek, for example – has a better understanding of the secrets of living tongues. To strive to give theoretical life to a long-dead tongue through the act of translation has a creative impact on our living language, especially our mother tongue. It gives us a sense of wonder about its life in the mouths of living humans, a wonder that it stretches voluptuously like breath itself, that it 'bursts from the hedge of his teeth' (Homer) and exhibits before us its syntactical articulations like a living, breathing organism, free from academic and grammatical sclerosis, lively and triumphant like an animal. The microscopic scrutiny of a dead language allows us to find the luminous logical skeleton beneath the opulence of the living tongue. It definitively helps to cultivate a writer's admiration for and joy in their instrument, without which it is impossible to craft a single page in which scientific sturdiness is united with verbal perfection, with a felicitous turn of phrase, the right image, the illuminating metaphor.

Marx's classical studies undoubtedly played a role in the development of his style. When these studies are truly fruitful, their effects cannot be reduced to erudition or to the discovery of 'eternal models'. On the contrary, their real value is exhibited in writers like Marx who acquire through them a profound understanding of the *living* language, a free taste for expressive perfection and for round phrasing. Valéry used to say this about the study of Greek, and Unamuno said the same for the study of Latin. Marx's precocious mastery of his own language, which shines brightly in his youthful writings (especially in those polished for publication as opposed to those which remain in draft form – a stylistic dichotomy which would endure for the length of his life), is due, in large part, to the formative linguistic effect of his study of the classics.

His first stylistic mode was that of metaphorical abundance. According to Cornu, the grader of the above-mentioned 'Reflections' noted that the text 'exhibited a great wealth of ideas, but often fell short in clarity of thought and stylistic correctness due to an excessive search for metaphors'.[7] Though Marx had to rein in his enthusiasm for metaphor for the rest of his life, brilliant traces of it appear in works such as the introduction to a *Critique of Hegel's Philosophy of Right*, *The Poverty of Philosophy*, *Wage Labour and Capital*, the *Critique of Political Economy* and *Capital*. Economic science – with its drive for precision and analysis – would frequently act as a moderating, equalizing force in this stylistic process. What remained was an irresistible metaphorical power controlled by, and in the service of, a theoretical-scientific framework. More profoundly, what would become a constitutive element of Marx's science was what we can call a *theoretical imagination*, a kind of scientific inspiration that, aided by formal precision, was always capable of reaching beyond social appearances for their structures, and beyond the theoretical postulates of political economy for their ideological underpinnings.

Marx, as we have noted, first considered himself a poet. There are two main reasons that allow us to easily demonstrate that this vocation was neither profound nor true, though it undoubtedly did help to shape his prose, since nothing gives shape to a prose style quite like the early practice of verse (prose itself often consisting of crouching verse). In the first place, Marx's poems were endearingly bad. While in literal despair over Jenny's refusals of his entreaties before their engagement became 'official', Marx filled three notebooks with poems, which he sent to his fiancée at Christmas 1836. They included a *Book of Songs* (*Buch der Lieder*) and a *Book of Love* (*Buch der Liebe*). He also wrote some sarcastic *Epigrams* and, in 1837, a few chapters of a novel, *Skorpion und Felix*, as well as the first scenes of a verse drama, *Oulanem*.

---

7 Cornu, *Karl Marx et Friedrich Engels: Leur vie et leur oeuvre*, tome I, p. 66.

The poems to Jenny have been evaluated by Mehring in no uncertain terms:

> They are completely formless in every sense of the word. The poetic technique is absolutely primitive and, if we did not know the precise dates in which they were written, no one could suspect that they were written a year after the death of Platen and nine years after the publication of Heine's *Book of Songs*. Beyond that, there is nothing forward-looking in their content. They are nothing more than the romantic sounds of a harp: elf songs, gnome songs, siren songs, songs to the stars, the song of the bell-ringer, the poet's last song, the pale maiden, the cycle of ballads of Albuin and Rosamunde.[8]

As for the novel, which Marx subtitled *A Humorous Novel*, it consisted of nothing more than crude jokes and aggressive jabs.

In his book *Marx, Engels and the Poets*, Peter Demetz is clear: 'The dilettante aspired to too much. In trying to imitate all the virtues of Sterne, Jean Paul, Hippel, and E. T. A. Hoffman in a single work, his efforts necessarily suffered from a lack of order, power, and effect.'[9] Marx recognized his own failure and, in an attempt to refashion himself, wrote his verse drama *Oulanem*, which, according to Demetz, 'followed closely the clichés of contemporary Gothic thriller'.[10]

What is most worth saving from this literary shambles (which, in being recognized as such, had a healthy and positive effect on

---

8   This passage is not from Mehring's biography of Marx but from Franz Mehring, *Aus dem literarschen Nachlass K. Marx, Fr. Engels*, Berlin, 1923, p. 26. [*Trans.*: I could not find an extant English translation of this text. This is my own translation that takes into account Silva's Spanish version and Cornu's French version.]

9   Peter Demetz, *Marx, Engels and the Poets*, University of Chicago Press, 1967, p. 52.

10   Demetz, *Marx, Engels and the Poets*, p. 54.

Marx in curing him of literature) is the *Epigrams*, which exhibit
the clear influence of Goethe and Schiller's celebrated *Xenions*
(1797). They are directed against Hegel. By efficiently deploying
rising hexameters, falling pentameters and quick cuts between
the two, they attempt to represent the movement of the dialectic.
Consider a brief example:

> Since I have found the Highest of things and the Depths of
>   them also,
> Rude am I as a God, cloaked by the dark like a God.
> Long have I searched and sailed on Thought's deep billowing
>   ocean;
> There I found me the Word: now I hold on to it fast.[11]

In the verses that follow we see some of the first manifestations
of something that becomes a fundamental feature of Marx's
expressive style: the play of contrasts, a kind of literary dialectic
of opposites. He says, for example: 'The Poet perceives what he
thinks, and thinks what he feels',[12] or, in a verse reminiscent of a
certain phrase of Saint John of God: 'Now you know all, since
I've said plenty of nothing to you!'[13]

Cornu gives an accurate, comprehensive evaluation of this
period:

> It is not the case that Karl Marx had no literary talent or
> poetic gift. He would, in the end, become a great writer whom
> one could compare to Lessing and Nietzsche for the precision

---

11   Marx, 'On Hegel', p. 576. 'Weil ich das Höchste entdeckt
und die Tiefe sinnend gefunden, / Bin ich grob, wie ein Gott, hüll'
mich in Dunkel, wie er. / Lange forscht' ich und trieb auf dem wogen-
den Meer der Gedanken, / Und da fand ich das Wort, halt' am
Gefundenen fest.'

12   Marx, 'On Hegel', p. 576. 'Und was er sinnet, erkennt, und was
er fühlet, ersinnt.'

13   Marx, 'On Hegel', p. 576. 'Alles sag' ich euch ja, weil ich Nichts euch
gesagt.'

and force of his style, the stunning beauty of his metaphors, and his delicate poetic sense, which eventually allowed him to become a much-loved – and much-feared – confidant of great poets such as Heinrich Heine and F. Freiligrath. But his soul was too unsettled and tormented then, his imagination too feverish.[14]

But perhaps the most accurate and precise judgement of his literary origins is the one Marx himself expressed in a letter to his father sent from Berlin on 10 November 1837, which shows his quick recovery from the literary syndrome of *Sturm und Drang*, already somewhat anachronistic by that time:

> In accordance with my state of mind at the time, lyrical poetry was bound to be my first subject, at least the most pleasant and immediate one. But owing to my attitude and whole previous development it was purely idealistic. My heaven, my art, became a world beyond, as remote as my love. Everything real became hazy and what is hazy has no definite outlines. All the poems of the first three volumes I sent to Jenny are marked by attacks on our times, diffuse and inchoate expressions of feeling, nothing natural, everything built out of moonshine, complete opposition between what is and what ought to be, rhetorical reflections instead of poetic thoughts, but perhaps also a certain warmth of feeling and striving for poetic fire.[15]

It is certainly symptomatic of the form of life and intellectual style of a man who was characterized by his radical and total critique of his contemporaries that he should have begun with such an accurate and incisive critique of himself.

---

14   Cornu, *Karl Marx et Friedrich Engels: Leur vie et leur oeuvre*, Vol. 1, p. 76.

15   'Letter from Marx to His Father', in *Karl Marx and Friedrich Engels Collected Works*, Vol. 1, p. 11.

And, in the end, there is a second group of reasons that ground our suspicions of his literary vocation. When he arrived in Bonn, Marx joined a group of young poets who gave readings and recitations. But what was the real activity of this unique club, given that it was promptly *levelled by the political police*?

2

The Fundamental Features of Marx's Style

So far, we have situated Marx's origins as a writer: his initiation and failure as a poet, which was, nevertheless, not a waste of time, given that verse is the best school for prose insofar as it allows for a deeper grasp of the plastic and rhythmic qualities of language, of prosody itself; his aesthetico-linguistic study of the classics, which made a decisive contribution to his consummate mastery of linguistic structure; his early passion for metaphorical idealization, which would eventually transform into the proper metaphorization of ideas; and, finally, his writerly self-criticism, which led him before the age of twenty – before even his start as a social scientist – to a mature mode of literary expression, to the intellectual style that always suited him.

We will now adopt a completely different vantage point. Taking Marx's oeuvre as a single expressive ensemble, a kind of vast musical score, we shall attempt to isolate some of the basic features that make up his intellectual and literary style.

The Architectonic of Science

Let us refer to the first stylistic feature, which is also the most general of them all, as the *architectonic of science* or the *scientific work as a work of art*.

We use the word 'architectonic' in the precise sense given to it by Kant in the final pages of his *Critique of Pure Reason*. Whatever position one adopts towards Kant's work, no one can reasonably doubt two things: that it is a monument to reason, and that it is stocked with valuable methodological observations, many of which still retain their usefulness. An example of both of these is the section entitled 'The Architectonic of Pure Reason'. There Kant writes:

> By an architectonic I mean the art of systems [*die Kunst der Systeme*]. Since systematic unity is that which first makes ordinary cognition into science . . . architectonic is the doctrine of that which is scientific in our cognition in general, and therefore necessarily belongs to the doctrine of method . . . For its execution the idea needs a schema, i.e., an essential manifoldness and order of the parts determined *a priori* from the principle of the end. A schema that is not outlined in accordance with an idea, i.e., from the chief end of reason, but empirically, in accordance with aims occurring contingently . . . yields *technical* unity, but that which arises only in consequence of an idea . . . grounds architectonic unity. What we call science, whose schema contains the outline (*monogramma*) and the division of the whole into members in conformity with an idea . . . arises architectonically.[16]

The art of constructing a system! What is scientific in our understanding is so because it possesses a systematic, architectonic unity in which all its parts correspond to one another and in which none is true without respect to the whole. Today, structuralism refers to this as 'the logical precedence of the whole to the parts', but in Kant the *a priori* was logico-transcendental, not merely logical. If we set aside the 'transcendental' implication, we are left with a perfectly valid methodological schema.

According to Kant, the architectonic is the *art* of systems. Here he is in agreement – and not by chance – with a great poet, Paul Valéry, who spoke of 'la plus poétique des idées: l'idée de

---

16   Immanuel Kant, *Critique of Pure Reason*, trans. Paul Guyer, Cambridge University Press, 1998, pp. 691–2.

composition'.[17] In this, Valéry was surely following in the steps of his equally great teacher Mallarmé, for whom each verse was *a musical score*, a minimal orchestra through which – to put it in the terms of everyone's teacher, Baudelaire – 'les parfums, les couleurs et les sons se répondent': they are architectonic 'correspondences'.

The general method of science and the general method of art thus coincide in this idea: for there to be science, and for there to be art, there must be architectonics. For thought to be science, it must be systematic; for expression to be art, it must be architectonic and be governed by the art of systems.

And if science implies architectonics, and architectonics implies art, then science implies art. This is the logical skeleton of this reasoning: if p implies q, and q implies r, then p implies r by the simple and clear law of transitivity. The material skeleton of this reasoning: if a structural condition of science is its architectonic character, and if, by the same token, a structural condition of art is its architectonic character, then science and art have at least one structural condition in common, 'r', which is a variable in the formal expression, and becomes a constant in the non-formal expression: the architectonic character.

Is it any wonder, then, that the architectonic dimension of a scientific system is also its beautiful side?

Karl Marx had a true lifelong obsession with constructing an *Economy* that had an architectonic structure and appearance. He was also conscious that this needed to be accomplished *in the same way as the creation of a work of art*. And not just in terms of the general form of the scientific edifice – its broadest and most general structural lines – but also in its smallest details: in the moulding of its expressions, the beadwork of its phrasing, the firm curves of its verbal vaults, in its metaphorical bas-relief, its conceptual pilasters and, in the end, its foundation in erudition.

Responding to Engels's insistence that the first volume of *Capital* be published at once, Marx replied: 'I cannot bring myself to

17   Paul Valéry, *Oeuvres*, Vol. 1, La Pléiade, 1957, p. 1504.

send anything off until I have the whole thing in front of me. Whatever shortcomings they may have, the advantage of my writings is that they are an artistic whole, and this can only be achieved through my practice of never having things printed until I have them in front of me *in their entirety*.'[18]

Note how Marx himself underlines the artistic and perfect 'whole' that his works needed to form before being sent to the press. What we refer to today as 'Marx's oeuvre' is divided into two great halves: what went to press during the author's lifetime and what was left incomplete in manuscript form. The first is the only part that can be considered 'finished' if we respect Marx's own literary and scientific criteria; it received the final burnishing of style, what Ortega refers to as 'the final rub of the pumice stone that buffs and braces'.[19] Following Marx's lead, we must consider the second half stylistically imperfect, incomplete, truncated. But was Marx right?

From the point of view of architectonics, he was clearly right. There is a stylistic abyss between the *Contribution to the Critique of Political Economy*, published in 1859, and the *Grundrisse*, drafted between 1857 and 1858. The comparison is even more appropriate once we realize that the *Critique* is a result of the investigations carried out in the *Grundrisse*. While he was writing the latter, Marx asked Lassalle to find him a publisher for his critical treatise on bourgeois political economy and capitalist society (the same old and gargantuan project he had painfully borne since 1844). Lassalle found Franz Duncker, who offered to pay good honoraria to Marx and so relieve his terrible poverty. The months pass and Lassalle does not receive a manuscript. In a letter of 22 October 1858, he conveys to Marx the editor's impatience, receiving the reply that, beyond poverty and disease of

---

18   'Marx to Engels, 31 July 1865', in *Karl Marx and Friedrich Engels Collected Works*, Vol. 42, Lawrence and Wishart, 2010, p. 173.

19   José Ortega y Gasset, 'Prólogo (to *Ideas y Crencias*)' in *Obras Completas de Ortega y Gasset*, Vol. 5, Revista de Occidente, 1964, p. 379.

the liver, Marx is delayed by 'preoccupations of style': the hepatic crises, he writes, leave their mark on the style of the work. Moreover, he explains, given that in his work 'an important view of social relations is scientifically expounded for the first time', its form must be perfect so that its literary expression matches this new conception.[20] It is only eight months later that the *Critique* appears in print. Despite having the manuscript of the *Grundrisse* at hand – a work of impressive quantitative and qualitative magnitude – Marx wrote a new work: the *Critique*. The other manuscript was left behind, never to be completed.

The experience of reading these two works is very different, which confirms the truth of what Marx affirmed in the above-cited letter to Engels – there are notable stylistic differences between the two. The *Grundrisse* is full of enormously long sentences filled with asides, parentheses, opacities, arbitrary mixtures of languages and other features that make the work difficult to read, despite the many brilliant and stylistically clear and finished passages it contains. The hand of a man in the throes of atrocious poverty (as he told it, bread and potatoes were all he ate at this time) is visible in the work. During the day, he was forced to write articles for the press as a kind of 'wage labour', and it was only at night that he could devote himself to what he called 'his true work'. He wrote feverishly until four in the morning, hoarding the time that slipped away from him, and, of course, without the peace or disposition necessary to polish what he wrote – or, better put, what trickled out of his brain. In terms of style, the *Critique* is something completely different. The existential poverty was the same, but at least while writing the *Critique* he had the promise of a few honoraria, thanks to which he was able to devote his 'waged labour time' to it and so create scientific and literary value during this time. In this way, Marx was able to concentrate all his gifts as a writer on

---

20   'Marx to Ferdinand de Lassalle in Berlin', in *Karl Marx and Friedrich Engels Collected Works*, Vol. 40, Lawrence and Wishart, 2010, p. 354.

this work. He was able to achieve a style that was cutting, incisive, ironic, full of round and polished phrases all consciously in
counterpoint to the work's conceptual clarity: in other words, a
complete union between the literary sign and the scientific
meaning. One can sit down to *read* the *Critique*; one must sit
down and *study* the *Grundrisse*. The latter is a brilliant draft, but
only a draft; the former, on the other hand, is one of the most
perfect models of scientific literature, of science as a work of art,
of scientific architectonics. As we shall see later, the same difference separates works like the *Critique of Hegel's Philosophy of
Right* from the *1844 Manuscripts*, or Volume 1 of *Capital* from
the *Theories of Surplus Value*.

This all means that we cannot consider Marx's oeuvre architectonically perfect in the same way as, say, the *Divine Comedy*.
However, if we abandon the point of view of totality and nail
down some partial perspectives, we can speak of one half of
Marx's works as being architectonically exemplary and stylistically rounded; that is, the part formed by the works he was able
to publish in his lifetime. In any case, Marx's plan was always
architectonic. In his edition of Marx's works,[21] Maximilien
Rubel has masterfully reconstructed the architecture of that
Economy that Marx always envisioned, starting in 1844 with
those first notebooks. The vastness of the project forced Marx to
abandon it periodically (notably in 1851–6, that time of poverty),
but in his correspondence he always promised to complete it.
Marx aspired to complete a scientific work that would encompass *every* aspect of his conception of history – those that he
schematically lays out in the celebrated Preface to the *Critique*
of 1859, and that include both the structural features of the
social edifice (*Struktur*) as well as the appearance of the structure itself (*Überbau*).[22] He eventually decided to concentrate all

---

21   Karl Marx, *Oeuvres: Économie*, ed. Maximilien Rubel, 1965
(Vol. 1) and 1968 (Vol. 2); cf. Vol. 2, pp. lxxxvi ff.
22   Cf. Karl Marx, 'Preface (to *A Contribution to the Critique of
Political Economy*)', in *Early Writings*, p. 424.

these plans in *Capital*, which was to comprise six books, of which he only 'finished' . . . one!

All those biographers who like to speak of the 'destiny' or 'pre-destination' of their subjects should know that, in Marx's case, there was no 'predestination' of any kind. Had there been, it surely would have kept Marx from so much acute misery, so many crises of the liver, so many boils, so much journalism, so many creditors who hounded him and forced him to hide like a hunted animal in Engels's house. Instead, it would have allowed him to finish many more works than he did, and to have completed many more parts of that vast architectonic edifice that he always hoped to erect.

The Expression of the Dialectic; the Dialectic of Expression

What we have called the *architectonic* character of Marx's intellectual style is what we might describe as a structural feature, discernible when his oeuvre is viewed as a whole. We will now invert our point of view and examine up close the verbal sinews that fill out and enliven that structural skeleton like a living mass of cells.

In so doing, we shall discover a new feature that is perhaps the most fundamental aspect of Marx's style. Adopting his manner, we might call this feature the *dialectic of expression* or, what comes to the same thing, the *expression of the dialectic*.

Marx is a dialectical materialist not just because he claimed to have isolated the 'rational kernel'[23] of the Hegelian dialectic and applied it to the study of history under the rubric of the material relations of production; he is also one because he materialized the dialectic in a literary style that is the most perfect expression of the logico-historical movement that makes up the dialectic.

---

23   Karl Marx, *Capital: Critique of Political Economy, Volume 1*, trans. Ben Fowkes, Penguin, 1992, p. 103.

No one, as far as we know, has noticed something that is out in the open: that Marx consciously sought to express – through certain particularities of literary style and through a specific verbal movement – the *real movement* to which his writings refer. In semantic-syntactical terms, the formal and logical relations into which Marx places verbal *signs/signifiers* constitute a plastic gesture intended to reflect the material and historical relations of *signifieds.*

The 'rational kernel' of the dialectic resides in a formula of Heraclitan provenance: the *coincidentia oppositorum*, the clash of opposites that produces a synthetic result. But it is impossible to understand Marx's dialectic if we stay with this formula. In pure logic, the negation of the negation is nothing more than a simple and direct affirmation. If we say 'not-not (p)', what we are really saying is simply 'p', just as in mathematics $[(2 - 2) + 2] = 2$. In Marx, that 'rational kernel' is nothing more than a *general guideline* for the theoretical expression of a real, historical movement. It can serve as a general guideline, but only on the condition that we do not attempt to use it with absolute logical precision – there is not, nor can there be, by our lights, a logical formulation of the real dialectical movement that is both 'materially adequate and formally correct' (Tarski).

So, for example, while it might be materially adequate to say (from the point of view of the classical theory of truth as *adaequatio* or correspondence), as Marx says, that the clash of historical antagonists (possessors and dispossessed, property owners and the expropriated) can produce a real historical synthesis whose future model is communist society in its higher stage, nevertheless, if we want to express that idea from a *strictly logical* and formally correct point of view, we could not claim that the clash of opposites 'produces' a synthesis; instead, we would have to speak of a *relation of conjunction* between opposites (that is: 'p and not-p') that could not result in any kind of 'dialectical' synthesis, since logical contradiction does not 'produce' anything, or, as Popper reminds us, produces anything:

(p and not-p) → (?)

The value of the relationship of implication (represented by '→') will always be tautological, will always be true, for whatever value we give the variable represented by the question mark. In logic, contradiction does not operate 'dialectically'. But this does not mean (as Popper erroneously hopes) that there are no real historical oppositions that can produce a synthesis. We can concede that, *stricto sensu*, it is inappropriate to speak of social 'contradictions' but still maintain that it is appropriate to speak of antagonism (Marx sometimes uses *Widerspruch* and at other times *Gegensatz*). *This is nothing more than proof that the strict application of the Hegelian logical schema to history has no place in Marx's plan* (as he proves so devastatingly in *The Poverty of Philosophy*). To claim otherwise would be to impute to Marx the Proudhonian ideology according to which history is governed by the Idea or ideas, by 'principles', rather than the other way around. What Marx actually does is point out the laws that concretely preside over the synthesis and the future overcoming of social antagonisms. As Mandel has noted, present-day society exhibits many concrete preconditions that herald this synthesis.

One of the aims of *The Poverty of Philosophy* is to destroy the Proudhonian illusion that Hegel's logical categories can be applied directly to political economy. Marx explained that such an application could only spawn a chimera: a metaphysics of political economy that would only ideologically mask the idealization and eternalization of capitalist material conditions – in other words, a metaphysical apologia for the system. Marx, who wrote the work in French so that Proudhon could understand it, writes:

> The abstraction of movement. What is the abstraction of movement? Movement in abstract condition. What is movement in abstract condition? The purely logical formula of movement or the movement of pure reason. Wherein does the

movement of pure reason consist? In posing itself, opposing itself, composing itself; in formulation itself as thesis, antithesis, synthesis; or, yet again, in affirming itself, negating itself and negating its negation. How does reason manage to affirm itself, to pose itself as a definite category? That is the business of reason itself and of its apologists.[24]

In this way, the movement of the dialectic, in its purely logical formulation, is nothing more than an abstraction, an abstract movement with no correspondence to reality. That peculiar *philosophy of history* that attempts to think of a reality in perfect correspondence to the logical schema is transformed, Marx notes with irony, into a *history of philosophy* simple and plain, an ideological history that conceals everything that might be of interest to political economy. Hence the attack on Proudhon and his *Système des contradictions*, a vain attempt to apply Hegel's logical categories directly to history (categories Proudhon did not understand well, and which Marx took it upon himself to explain to him). Proudhon committed the same egregious error as today's Marxist commissar-philosophers, who form a praetorian guard around the 'three laws of dialectics' and transform Marx into the most shameless Hegelian idealist – there is no doubt that they have failed to read the wholly unambiguous passages of *The Poverty of Philosophy*. For Marx, the dialectic was not a strictly

---

24   Karl Marx, 'The Poverty of Philosophy: Answer to the *Philosophy of Poverty* by M. Proudhon', in *Karl Marx and Friedrich Engels Collected Works*, Vol. 6, Lawrence and Wishart, 2010, p. 164; 'Misère de la philosophie (Réponse à la "Philosophie de la misère" de M. Proudhon)', in Marx, *Oeuvres*, Vol. 1, p. 77: 'L'abstraction du mouvement. Qu'est-ce que l'abstraction du mouvement? Le mouvement à l'état abstrait. Qu'est-ce que le mouvement à l'état abstrait? La formule purement logique du mouvement ou le mouvement de la raison pure. En quoi consiste le mouvement de la raison pure? A se poser, à s'opposer, à se composer, à se formuler comme thèse, antithèse, synthèse, ou bien encore à s'affirmer, à se nier, à nier sa négation. Comment fait-elle, la raison, pour s'affirmer, pour se poser en catégorie déterminée? C'est l'affaire de la raison elle-même et de ses apologistes.'

logical method; it was a historical method. For a logical method to be formally correct it must be empty, but Marx was interested precisely in the fullness of history, in its concrete multiplicity.

> Let us admit with M. Proudhon that real history, history according to the order in time, is the historical sequence in which ideas, categories and principles have manifested themselves. Each principle has had its own century in which to manifest itself. The principle of authority, for example, had the eleventh century, just as the principle of individualism had the eighteenth century. In logical sequence, it was the century that belonged to the principle, and not the principle that belonged to the century. In other words, it was the principle that made the history, and not the history that made the principle.[25]

This passage is so explicit that it's worth citing in full, not just because it confirms our claims, but because it serves as a perfect illustration of the stylistic feature we'll seek to define. Marx continues:

> When, consequently, in order to save principles as much as to save history, we ask ourselves why a particular principle was manifested in the eleventh or in the eighteenth century rather than in any other, we are necessarily forced to examine minutely what men were like in the eleventh century, what they were like in the eighteenth, what were their respective

---

25   Marx, 'The Poverty of Philosophy', p. 170. 'Admettons avec M. Proudhon que l'histoire réelle, l'histoire selon l'ordre des temps, est la succession historique dans laquelle les idées, les catégories, les principes se sont manifestés. Chaque principe a eu son siècle, pour s'y manifester: le principe d'autorité, par exemple, a eu le XI° siècle, de même que le principe d'individualisme le XVIII° siècle. De conséquence en conséquence, c'était le siècle qui appartenait au principe, et non le principe qui appartenait au siècle. En d'autres termes, c'était le principe qui faisait l'histoire, ce n'était pas l'histoire qui faisait le principe.'

needs, their productive forces, their mode of production, the
raw materials of their production – in short, what were the
relations between man and man which resulted from all these
conditions of existence. To get to the bottom of all these questions – what is this but to draw up the real, profane history of
men in every century and to present these men as both the
authors and the actors of their own drama? But the moment
you present men as the actors and authors of their own
history, you arrive – by a detour – at the real starting point,
because you have abandoned those eternal principles of which
you spoke at the outset.[26]

This digression on the dialectic was necessary in order to
pre-empt the accusation that I am engaged in a Proudhonian
literary mystification of the dialectic. When I say that Marx's
style is a living expression of his dialectics, I am not reaching for
profundity, nor am I suggesting that rigid and mysterious logical
schemas are hidden in Marx's sentences or that these sentences
contain a mythological Hegelian Spirit. All I am doing is point-
ing out a stylistic feature which was clearly consciously developed
by Marx. The 'dialectical' label that I affix to Marx's style is not

26   Marx, 'The Poverty of Philosophy', p. 170. Marx, 'Misère de la
philosophie', p. 93: 'Lorsque, ensuite, pour sauver les principes autant
que l'histoire, on se demande pourquoi tel principe s'est manifesté dans
le XI° ou dans le XVIII° siècle plutôt que dans tel autre, on est néces-
sairement forcé d'examiner minutieusement quels étaient les hommes
du XI° siècle, quels étaient ceux du XVIII°, quels étaient leurs besoins
respectifs, leurs forces productrices, leur mode de production, les
matières premières de leur production, enfin quels étaient les rapports
d'homme à homme qui résultaient de toutes ces conditions d'existence.
Approfondir toutes ces questions, n'est-ce pas faire l'histoire réelle,
profane des hommes dans chaque siècle, représenter ces hommes à la
fois comme les auteurs et les acteurs de leur propre drame? Mais du
moment que vous représentez les hommes comme les acteurs et les
auteurs de leur propre histoire, vous êtes, par un détour, arrivé au
véritable point de départ, puisque vous avez abandonné les principes
éternels dont vous parliez d'abord.'

a strictly *logical* label. But that does not mean that there are no objective reasons for describing it this way.

The literary secret behind how 'rounded' and striking so many of Marx's sentences are is also the secret behind his dialectical conception of history as class struggle or a struggle of opposites. His sentences very frequently exhibit a syntactical structure in which the opposite terms are neatly drawn in an antagonistic correlation before being fused in a synthetic phrase. We have just seen this in the passage cited above: 'it was the century that belonged to the principle, and not the principle that belonged to the century. In other words, it was the principle that made the history, and not the history that made the principle.'

The literary secret that governs these constructions is commonly found in the work of great prose stylists and, especially, in the work of great poets (Petrarch and Garcilaso, for example). It involves formulating a phrase and then following it up with another that says the inverse but that *uses the same words with inverted syntax*, and then, frequently, finishing it all off with a third phrase that also uses the same words but that adds some new ones, thereby constituting a *synthesis* of the previously established antagonistic correlations. In speaking of 'correlations', we are thinking of the literary theory of correlations formulated by the Spanish philologist Dámaso Alonso and by disciples of his like Carlos Bousoño,[27] according to which many poems both classical and modern contain a structure of metaphorical correlations that first names a set of objects, then names a set of metaphorical correspondences to those objects, and that finally brings them all together – the objects and their correspondences – in a final synthetic phrase. Marx's sentences often do the same, and that is why they so often appear to be stylistically well rounded. But because Marx often engages in a play of conceptual oppositions reflected in the play of verbal and

---

27 See Dámaso Alonso and Carlos Bousoño, *Seis calas en la expresión literaria española* [*Six Stages in Spanish Literary Expression*], Gredo, 1951, chapters 2, 3, and 4 in particular.

syntactical oppositions, it would not be inaccurate to describe this practice as genuinely dialectical.

Note, for example, the following fragment from the *1844 Manuscripts*:

> How could the product of the worker's activity confront him as something alien if it were not for the fact that in the act of production he was estranging himself from himself? After all, the product is simply the résumé of the activity, of the production. So if the product of labour is alienation, production itself must be active alienation, the alienation of activity, the activity of alienation. The estrangement of the object of labour merely summarizes the estrangement, the alienation in the activity of labour itself.[28]

We have sought to preserve in translation the key features of Marx's style, as well as the elaborate and precise wordplay that is, of course, much more than mere play.[29]

---

28   Marx, 'Economic and Philosophical Manuscripts (1844)', in *Early Writings*, p. 326. Karl Marx, *Oekonomisch-philosophische Manuskripte aus dem Jahre 1844*, in *Marx-Engels Werke*, 'Ergänzungsband: Schriften bis 1844, erster Teil', p. 514: 'Wie würde der Arbeiter dem Produkt seiner Tätigkeit fremd gegenübertreten können, wenn er im Akt der Produktion selbst sich nicht sich selbst entfremdete? Das Produkt ist ja nur das Resümee der Tätigkeit, der Produktion. Wenn also das Produkt der Arbeit die Entäußerung ist, so muß die Produktion selbst die tätige Entäußerung, die Entäußerung der Tätigkeit, die Tätigkeit der Entäußerung sein. In der Entfremdung des Gegenstandes der Arbeit resümiert sich nur die Entfremdung, die Entäußerung in der Tätigkeit der Arbeit selbst.'

29   We do, however, find it necessary to unify Marx's vocabulary by adopting a practice, common also among French Marxists, of using 'alienation' to refer to the reality that Marx names with three different words that alternate in his youthful writings (in his mature writings, he almost always uses 'Entfremdung'). [*Trans.*: In the present context, to preserve Marx's wordplay, we follow Livingstone and Benton in translating 'Entfremdung' as 'estrangement' and 'Entäusserung' as 'alienation', without attempting to establish subtle differences between the English terms.]

This fragment demonstrates the feature that we previously attempted to explicate theoretically. The oppositions here, however, are not conceptual but merely verbal. In order to say the same thing, note how Marx exhausts every syntactical possibility: 'the product of labour is alienation, production itself must be active alienation, the alienation of activity'. There is a virtuosic linguistic move between the first 'determination' of the estrangement of labour (the estrangement of the product) and the second (the estrangement of the activity of production). The conceptual move is reflected in a very expressive formal pirouette. From another angle, we can also see the structure of the correlations that end up fused together that we discussed above. The key terms – 'product', 'estrangement–alienation' and 'production-activity of production' – are first introduced interrogatively, are then affirmed, and are finally recapitulated in the closing phrase in which the conceptual and formal moves are both consummated.

The passage that follows the one we have been discussing is equally significant, because in it the play of opposites is very clearly, even linearly, drawn. To aid the reader, we will attempt to display these oppositions graphically:

Worin besteht nun die Entäußerung der Arbeit?
What, then, constitutes the alienation of labour?

Erstens, daß die Arbeit dem Arbeiter
äußerlich *ist*   *d. h. nicht zu seinem Wesen gehört*

Firstly, the fact that labour is *external* i.e. does not belong to his essential being;
to the worker,

daß er sich daher in seiner Arbeit nicht
bejaht   *sondern verneint*

that he therefore does not confirm
himself in his work,   but denies himself,

nicht wohl   *sondern unglücklich fühlt*
feels miserable,   and not happy,

keine freie physische und geistige
Energie entwickelt   *sondern seine Physis abkasteit und seinen*
                                            Geist ruiniert.

does not develop free mental and
physical energy   but mortifies his flesh and ruins his mind.

Der Arbeiter fühlt sich daher erst
außer der Arbeit bei sich   *und in der Arbeit außer sich.*

Hence the worker feels himself only   when he is working he does not feel
when he is not working;   himself.

Zu Hause ist er, wenn er nicht arbeitet, *und wenn er arbeitet, ist er nicht zu Haus.*
He is at home when he is not working,   and not at home when he is working.

Seine Arbeit ist daher nicht freiwillig, *sondern gezwungen,* Zwangsarbeit.
His labour is therefore not voluntary,   but forced; it is *forced labour.*

Sie ist daher nicht die Befriedigung
eines Bedürfnisses,   *sondern sie ist nur ein* Mittel, *um*
                                             Bedürfnisse außer ihr zu befriedigen.
It is therefore not the satisfaction of but a mere means to satisfy needs outside
a need;   itself.

[. . .] *Wie in der Religion die Selbst-*
tätigkeit der menschlichen Phantasie,
des menschlichen Hirns und des
menschlichen Herzens unabhängig
vom Individuum, d. h. als eine fremde,
göttliche oder teuflische Tätigkeit, auf
es wirkt,   *so ist die Tätigkeit des Arbeiters nicht*
                                             seine Selbsttätigkeit. Sie gehört einem
[. . .] **Just as in religion the spontane-** *andren, sie ist der Verlust seiner selbst.*
ous activity of the human
imagination, the human brain and the
human heart detaches itself from the
individual and reappears as the alien
activity of a god or of a devil,

                                             so the activity of the worker is not his
                                             own spontaneous activity. It belongs to
                                             another, it is a loss of his self.[30]

---

30   Marx, 'Economic and Philosophical Manuscripts (1844)', pp. 326–7.

We could continue quoting, because this section of the *1844 Manuscripts* is filled with many such oppositions, all of which have the purpose of delineating the moral, psychological and even physiological effects of alienated labour. If alienation is, at its root, a kind of separation of the self, a *splitting*, what better way to express it stylistically than through the splitting of sentences into pairs of linear oppositions? Moreover, the condition of doubling must be stylistically synthesized, hence the comparison to religion – which, it bears saying, is very frequent in Marx – and also the comparison to animal life, as if the point were to paint man as profoundly riven across the whole distance that separates beasts from gods. This is why Marx says that the worker, who is a man, feels free in his animal functions, and feels like an animal in his human functions; he feels free when he eats, drinks and sleeps, he feels like an animal when he works; therefore, to sum up: *Tierische wird das Menschliche und das Menschliche das Tierische* – what is animal becomes human and what is human becomes animal.[31]

Marx employs this same stylistic mode in *The Holy Family* in order to describe class antagonism. If a real antagonism exists between the propertied and dispossessed classes, it must also be verbally reflected through oppositions. The reader should try to read the following excerpt in the same way as the one quoted above:

(a) The propertied class and the class of the proletariat present the same human self-estrangement.

(b) But the former class feels at ease and strengthened in this self-estrangement, it recognizes estrangement as *its own power* and has in it the *semblance* of a human existence.

---

31   Marx, 'Economic and Philosophical Manuscripts (1844)', p. 327. Marx, *Oekonomisch-philosophische Manuskripte aus dem Jahre 1844*, in *Marx-Engels Werke*, p. 515.

(c) The class of the proletariat feels annihilated in estrangement; it sees in it its own powerlessness and the reality of
an inhuman existence.[32]

We have divided this passage into three parts in order to highlight its absolute stylistic precision and its play of correspondences.
Section (a) introduces the topic; in (b) we find 'feels at ease',
'strengthened', 'its own power', 'semblance' and 'human existence'; in (c), on the contrary, we find – in perfect negative
correspondence with (b) – 'feels annihilated', ['negated',] 'powerlessness', 'reality' and 'inhuman existence'. Now, this play of
opposites does not remain immutable, but is instead fused, synthesized in the claim that both antagonistic elements form
definite parts of the same human self-estrangement. They form a
whole, an entire social structure based on class antagonism, like
a sphere with two opposite poles. The private property owner,
Marx tells us in the same place, represents the action that preserves this antithesis; at the same time, the proletarian represents
the action of its destruction – a conservative force squares off
against a subversive force. (Following Mannheim, we could add:
a realized ideology faces a realizable utopia.) Such is the real historical movement, full of contradictions whose development will
yield their own dialectical solutions. Marx explains this theory
in simple terms in *Capital* when he writes:

We saw in a former chapter that the exchange of commodities implies contradictory and mutually exclusive conditions.
The further development of the commodity does not abolish
these contradictions, but rather provides the form within
which they have room to move. This is, in general, the way in
which real contradictions are resolved. For instance, it is a
contradiction to depict one body as constantly falling towards

---

32   Karl Marx and Friedrich Engels, 'The Holy Family, or Critique
of Critical Criticism', in *Karl Marx and Friedrich Engels Collected
Works*, Vol. 4, Lawrence and Wishart, 2010, p. 37.

another and at the same time constantly flying away from it. The ellipse is a form of motion within which this contradiction is both realized and resolved.[33]

Marx's entire oeuvre is filled with sentences like the ones we have just analysed. This is the literary expression, rendered with the greatest artistic care, of a mind that saw capitalist society as a nursery of objective contradictions: Capital v. Labour, Appropriation v. Alienation, Bourgeoisie v. Proletariat, Ideology v. Class-Consciousness, Market Needs v. Human Needs, Exchange-Value v. Use-Value, Relations of Production v. Relations of Destruction, Social Structure v. Social Appearance, Division of Labour v. Division of the Labourer, the Socialization of Production v. the Private Mode of Appropriation and so on.

The objective existence and uncovering of these contradictions (which do not represent, as people like Popper suggest,[34] the 'forces of evil' versus the 'forces of good', or a 'conspiracy theory' but, rather, human history itself, its 7,000 years of exploitation) are what truly make Marx's thought dialectical. The dialectic in Marx is not a Hegelian super-Reason implicit in history; it is nothing more and nothing less than a rational method for looking at history from the point of view of the class struggle and the relations of production. As we saw in a text above, it is not a question of explaining history through principles or ideas but of explaining principles or ideas through history. Marx did not confuse the rational and the real; he was not the pan-logician celebrated by those who try to make the Marxian dialectic a method for explaining every topic in the universe. The dialectic is simply the Marxist method for the study of history.

His style was true to his thought. Perhaps with the examples we have quoted and analysed we have been able to give a sense of

---

33   Marx, *Capital, Volume 1*, p. 198.
34   Cf. Karl Popper, *Conjectures and Refutations: The Growth of Scientific Knowledge*, Routledge, 2002, pp. 165–6.

this fundamental feature of Marx's style. We could multiply the quotations, but that is unnecessary in this essay, which only seeks to point out fields for the study of this virtually undiscussed aspect of Marx's work.

What is certain is that the principal feature of Marx's literary style is the elaborate and conscious correspondence of its conceptual contents. We have sought out the most perfect expression of this correspondence in certain representative passages in which the dialectical play of opposites is clear and in which the sign-meaning correspondence is neatly drawn. That said, this correspondence is expressed in Marx's oeuvre in a thousand different ways – this is merely the most obvious and constant. Marx has an infinite capacity for adapting his style to his objects of study, and he preserves, over the course of his life's work, a curious uniformity in the vocabulary he deploys to refer to certain topics. Althusser claims that it is possible to detect in *Capital* the presence of a *theoretical praxis* that, if analysed, would constitute the secret of Marxist dialectics and epistemology. There is no doubt that one of the conditions for unearthing that theoretical praxis is the analysis of Marx's literary form, which reflects with unbelievable precision the real, historical movements to which his words refer. It is definitely not a style that is happy to 'designate' phenomena; it is instead a style that also *represents* them, that performs them, as if the words were suddenly transformed into actors on a stage. In this sense, Marx's language is the *theatre* of his dialectic.

Plato writes in the *Cratylus*: 'probably the best possible way to speak consists in using names all (or most) of which are most like the things they name (that is, are appropriate to them), while the worst is to use the opposite kind of names'.[35]

---

35   Plato, *Cratylus*, 432 c6–d1.

Marx's Great Metaphors

Over the course of Marx's oeuvre, we can see the consistent, periodic reappearance of certain great metaphors: matrix-metaphors that encompass all of his other literary figures and that serve as their totality. They are the metaphors with which he illustrates his conception of history and they also often allow him to formulate his implacable criticism of bourgeois ideologues and economists.

One would need an entire volume to study the most important of these vast metaphors in detail. They do not play a merely literary or ornamental role in Marx's work; beyond their aesthetic value, they achieve a cognitive value as the expressive support of his science. Those who believe that metaphors are not a source of knowledge are wrong; metaphors may not represent exact knowledge, but they have a cognitive value. The foundation of any metaphor is analogical reasoning, and ever since Aristotle we have known that we understand many things by analogy, which he defined as 'equality of shares'.[36] To establish the equal shares that exist between two sets of phenomena (for example, between the lungs and the air and gills and water) is to take an important step in the study of these phenomena. Along with these reasons are those wielded by the poets: every suitable metaphor expands the expressive power of language, and every science needs a powerfully expressive language; therefore, every appropriate metaphor is an excellent companion to science, just as all appropriate examples are. As Nietzsche affirmed, when it comes to expressing a thought, sometimes metaphors and examples are everything.

We will only examine three of Marx's great metaphors here: 1) the 'superstructure' metaphor; 2) the 'reflection' metaphor; and 3) the metaphor of religion. We can still, however, point out

---

36 Aristotle, *Nicomachean Ethics*, 1131 A31: ἡ γὰρ ἀναλογία ἰσότης ἐστὶ λόγων.

others that are no less important. What is the famous 'commodity fetishism', for example, if not a gigantic metaphor, set like a diamond in the frame of a scientific theory in order to make it more expressive and comprehensible? The theory that holds that the fundamental social relations in society – which are human productive relations – appear as relations between *things* (including capitalism itself, which is nothing more than a social relation but which appears as a thing, a thing so thoroughly mysterious that it is even capable of 'generating' more capital, as happens with usury capitalism and finance capital more generally) finds its perfect analogy in the primitive phenomenon of commodity fetishism, whose essential feature is the personification of a thing – the fetish – that it endows with the power to dispose of life and death. It therefore also implies the thingification of the person prostrate before the fetish, full of fear and owing his own life to it. The worker is worth nothing to the capitalist as a person; his only *value* is as a commodity. At the same time, the commodity produced by the worker is transformed for him into the authentic fetish to which he owes his life, that is, his means of living ('You take my life / When you do take the means whereby I live' – lines from Shakespeare that Marx was fond of citing).[37] This is what Marx called the 'alienation of the product' or the dominion of the product over the producer. In general, economic life becomes the dominion of things. Money is a social relation, but appears as a thing that dominates every social relation. Time becomes gold, that is, coin or the 'general equivalent' (labour *time* effectively becomes the creator of monetary wealth!). In turn, things become persons: 'as soon as it emerges as a commodity, it changes into a thing which transcends sensuousness. It not only stands with its feet on the ground, but, in relation to all other commodities, it stands on its head, and evolves out of its wooden brain grotesque ideas, far more wonderful than if it were to begin dancing of its own free will.'[38]

---

37   For example in Marx, *Capital*, Vol. 1, p. 618.
38   Ibid., pp. 163–4.

In his fascinating work *The Golden Bough*, Frazer recounts that on the island of Timor (in the East Indies) there are two types of chief. The first is the 'civil rajah', a type of 'civil chief' in charge of directing political matters; the second is a *chief fetish* or 'fetish chief'[39] in charge – by mere chance? – of everything related to the *economy* and to the community's means of subsistence. By form and appearance, the first of these chiefs is the more important; but in real, material terms, it is the fetish chief who decides on truly important and vital matters, basic matters, economic matters. His principal power involves 'declaring anything taboo'.[40] What is a reality *sans phrase* among these primitive peoples is what Marx refers to as fetishism in modern capitalist nations. In these, a state manages politics and its powers are supposedly the most important. But the truly important and vital functions, the basic or economic functions, are managed by a fetish chief: capital, adorned by feathers and subtleties such as 'use-values', 'exchange-values', 'wages', 'labour-power', 'the monetary system' and so on. The true name of 'anonymous' firms is the *capital* they possess, and it is a name they cannot hide behind any kind of anonymity, because it is their true name. The relations between capitalist X and capitalist W are not relations between people but, rather, between capitals. This supreme modern fetish acquires so much personality that, when placed in a bank, absent the immediate presence of its owners, it fructifies and grows through interest. In the same manner, the 'relations of production' do not appear as the relations between a capitalist and a worker, but as the relations that obtain between a capital and a labour-power as a *commodity* – this is why Marx says that 'capital employs labour'. And, while labour has produced capital, it has done so the way primitive man produces his fetish by hand, that is, as an object that in the future, after it has been created or produced, will become the master and lord of the

39   [*Trans.*: 'fetish king' in Frazer's original.]
40   James George Frazer, *The Golden Bough: A Study in Magic and Religion*, Palgrave Macmillan, 1990, pp. 78, 86.

creator or producer. We are not in a primitive state, which is why we cannot speak of *real* fetishism; nevertheless, fetishism is the most appropriate metaphor for illustrating the true character of the social relations that obtained in Marx's time and that still obtain, even more so, today.

But let us turn to the three great metaphors we have promised to analyse. And let us do so carefully, because it will be very difficult, if not impossible, to separate them, as stylistic features, from Marx's whole conceptual framework.

'Superstructure' as Metaphor

At the outset, this topic presents us with a tremendous difficulty. To treat what the great majority of Marxists, Marxologists and Marxians consider to be a complete scientific *explanation* as a metaphor – or, more accurately, as an analogy that grounds a great metaphor – can easily sound like heresy, or like a 'bourgeois subtlety' meant to undermine Marx's theoretical edifice. Moreover, to engage polemically with the distinct number – small though it may be – of authors who see 'superstructure' as a scientific explanation and not a metaphor would take us so far afield that we would have to abandon our goal of discussing Marx's style and turn our essay into an exercise in Marxist theory. We will nevertheless have to hazard such an incursion into this way of thinking, among other things because with Marx, as with any author of scientific theories, it is absolutely impossible to separate out *signs* from *meanings* (signifieds), or, as was once said in an aestheticizing vein, 'form' from 'content'.

A truly *literary* style exists where signs express meanings most exactly – plastically, musically, and in terms of prosody; that is, where there is no dissonance or disproportion between the signs deployed and their intended meanings. As Antonio Machado said, to say what happens in the street, one must say 'what happens in the street', or something like it – 'what happens in the street every day', for instance; one should never say 'the customary events that transpire in the thoroughfare'. This last example exhibits dissonance or disproportion: in it, there is an absence of agreement between sign and meaning. There is no style; the verbal scalpel's incision on the conceptual torso is not exact. If a writer like Marx has style, and a brilliant style at that, it is because, in his prose, signs and meanings march in tandem, in a balance of forces, and together can engage in any number of pirouettes, just as consummate athletes with perfectly calibrated weights, powers and movements can accomplish aerial feats that, for all their daring, do not contravene the laws of physics but rather play with them.

What in learned Spanish is referred to as 'superstructure' – sometimes turned into 'supra-structure', or, more sensibly, 'over-structure' – Marx designated in two ways. Sometimes, employing a Latin etymology, he says *Superstruktur*; in others, employing a German one, he says *Überbau*, which literally refers to the upper (*über*) part of a building or structure (*Bau*). In strict architectural terms, however, it is not appropriate to use *Überbau* or super-structure to refer to the upper part of a building – the whole thing is, after all, a single structure. *Überbau* really refers to the scaffolding or framework that is attached to a building during its construction and that is, logically, removed upon completion. An architectonically complete building is a structure, with no trace of superstructure, *Überbau*, or scaffolding.

Neither of the above-mentioned words appears with any frequency in Marx's writings, contrary to what one might infer from so much of the literature on ideological superstructures. It is true that Engels does insist on the term – in some letters from the 1880s in particular – but Marx only mentions it on very rare occasions.

As far as we remember, Marx employs *Superstruktur* only three times and *Überbau* only once. We might well be wrong about these numbers, but, in any case, it is clear that Marx hardly ever used these expressions. This is the first reason for thinking that, while it may illustrate a scientific theory, *for Marx* the famous 'superstructure' was nothing more than a metaphor, used with stylistic discretion on a couple of occasions but more often replaced by other metaphors or, better yet, *theoretical explanations*. The same is true of the equally famous 'reflection', a metaphor arbitrarily turned into a theory that we will examine later. When Marx got hold of a *theory*, he analysed it and repeated it to the point of exhaustion, as happens with the theory of labour-power or the theory of surplus-value. On the other hand, when he employed a metaphor, he knew to be discreet and he used it on few occasions, because he was well aware that metaphors, when used properly, demand the strictest stylistic economy.

Let us turn to the texts. In *The German Ideology* Marx writes:

> The form of intercourse determined by the existing productive forces at all previous historical stages, and in its turn determining these, is *civil society* . . . [it] has as its premise and basis the simple family and the multiple, called the tribe . . . Already here we see that this civil society is the true focus and theatre of all history, and how absurd is the conception of history held hitherto, which neglects the real relations and confines itself to spectacular historical events.
>
> [. . .]
>
> Civil society embraces the whole material intercourse of individuals within a definite stage of the development of productive forces . . . The term 'civil society' [*bürgerliche Gesellschaft*] emerged in the eighteenth century, when property relationships had already extricated themselves from the ancient and medieval communal society. Civil society as such only develops with the bourgeoisie; the social organisation evolving directly out of production and intercourse, which in all ages forms the basis [*Basis*] of the state and of the rest of the idealistic superstructure [*idealistischen Superstruktur*], has, however, always been designated by the same name.[41]

41   Karl Marx and Friedrich Engels, 'The German Ideology', in *Karl Marx and Friedrich Engels Collected Works*, Vol. 5, Lawrence and Wishart, 2010, pp. 50, 89.

This fragment is the most exact prefiguration of the historical-materialist design laid out by Marx in his famous Preface of 1859, which we will examine later. Now, that 'superstructure' to which the text refers – is it an explanation or a metaphor? If it were an explanation, it would have to make explicit the concrete way in which social, material relations – the 'civil society' of which Hegel spoke – produce ad hoc ideological formations: legal bodies that use tortuous casuistry to justify private property as an 'inalienable right' (!); religious beliefs that give celestial foundations to earthly misery by extolling the wonders of material poverty; phenomena like the state which, while *products* of specific material situations, constitute themselves as *producers* and preservers of those situations; and, finally, the celebrated 'principles' of the philosophers, products of history which identify themselves as its motors. None of this is explained with the mere mention of a 'superstructure' built upon a 'base'. In other parts of *The German Ideology* – as well as in other works of his – Marx gives us explanations like the ones alluded to above, but it is *precisely then*, when he moves to *explain*, that he abandons the metaphor of the 'superstructure' and dedicates himself to giving detailed explanations of ideological formations and their relationships to the structure of society.

Marx knew what Marxists seem to ignore: that it's one thing to give a schematic introduction to a theory by means of illustrative metaphors and quite another to explain that same theory scientifically and positively. Precisely because his work goes beyond pure metaphor, Marx was well within his rights as a writer when he employed metaphors in the sense we have noted. The same thing happens with *alienation*, which began as an ethical metaphor and progressively became a socio-economic explanation. The claim that the worker is 'alienated from himself' is, at first, a metaphor; it turns into an explanation when, guided by Marx, we realize that in becoming a *commodity* (as it must due to the social regime of production), the worker's labour-power becomes the worker's own worst enemy.

Just as there are those who make tendentious attempts to reduce alienation to its metaphorical qualities and speak of a phantom 'human essence' that is separated from the worker (and in so doing arbitrarily reduce Marx's entire corpus to a few passages from the *1844 Manuscripts* that Marx never authorized), there is a whole legion of ostensible Marxists who reduce the theory of ideological formations to the pure metaphor of the 'ideological superstructure', a metaphor that, isolated from the whole theoretical *designatum* which it is meant to merely *illustrate*, flips Marx's whole theory on its head and leaves upside down everything he worked so hard to put on firm ground. Well, let us suppose, for a moment, that 'superstructure' is an explanatory and not merely a metaphorical term – what would it 'explain' to us? It can explain no more than the following: society, as a material structure, has an ideal superstructure *constructed* upon itself; but, if this superstructure is constructed in the same way as a scaffolding, it can be separated from the structure – all scaffolding can be removed, after all – and can thus be considered an independent entity. If ideology is *truly*, and not just metaphorically, a 'superstructure', what prevents us from taking it as its own celestial body, as an autonomous framework? Which puts us in precisely the same position as the ideologues whom Marx so relentlessly attacked – did he not reproach them for thinking of ideas, beliefs, religions and philosophical 'postulates' as realms apart that exist independently of civil society, that is, of the material life of society? Is this not precisely why he called them *ideologues*?

In other words, to accept 'superstructure' as a scientific explanation is to turn Marx himself into an *ideologue*, if not into a shameless Platonist believer in a *topos hyperouranios*, in a home for the ideas found beyond the sky.

Let us now look at the famous passage from Marx's Preface to his *Contribution to the Critique of Political Economy* (1859), which is embraced with a bear-like grip by all of those whom, following García Bacca, we'll call 'dogmantiquers':

> In the social production of their existence, men inevitably enter into definite relations, which are independent of their will, namely relations of production appropriate to a given stage in the development of their material forces of production. The totality of these relations of production constitutes the economic structure of society [*ökonomische Struktur*], the real foundation [*die reale Basis*], on which arises a legal and political superstructure [*Überbau*] and to which correspond definite forms of social consciousness . . . The changes in the economic foundation [*ökonomische Grundlage*] lead sooner or later to the transformation of the whole immense superstructure. [Mit der Veränderung der ökonomischen Grundlage wälzt sich der ganze ungeheure Überbau langsamer oder rascher um.][42]

As is widely known, the French translation of Volume 1 of *Capital* by J. Roy was personally revised by Marx himself. Now, in Volume 1, Marx quotes the fragment of his Preface of 1859 that we have transcribed above. We can suppose that, given the importance of this text, Marx must have granted it extra attention in his revision. In the French version, *Überbau* is not given as 'superstructure' but as 'edifice' (*édifice*), and *Basis* and *Grundlage* are translated as *fondation*.

No one will deny, sensibly at least, that these terms possess greater authority than the much-touted 'base' and 'superstructure' that contemporary Marxism talks so much about. But our goal here is not to lock ourselves into a merely terminological question. Mostly for the worse, 'base' and 'superstructure' tend to say the same thing as the other terms, in the sense that they can play a role as terms in an analogy. But they fulfil this role less successfully, from the literary point of view, because Marx's point is to compare the economic structure of society to the foundations of a building on the one hand, and, on the other,

---

42   Marx, 'Preface (to *A Contribution to the Critique of Political Economy*)', pp. 425–6.

to compare that society's ideological formation (that is, its legal
and political 'façade' – the 'state') to the building itself, which
rests on those foundations. An *ideologue* is one who, with crude
provincial reasoning, thinks that if the foundations are not visible, they must not exist; that is, one who confuses society with its
legal-political façade, forgetting or denying – like an intellectual
ostrich – the real economic groundwork that sustains the whole
façade. And, if he sees an inverted world, with his head on the
ground, it is because he believes that the building holds up
the foundation, and not the other way around – he judges societies according to what they think about themselves, by the
intellectual clothing they wear, and not by the real relations
sustained by the individuals who make them up. This takes on
an exceedingly concealing and misleading cast as soon as one
thinks of these relations as relations of exploitation.

The analogy, then, runs as follows:

$$\frac{\text{The Economic Structure } (Struktur)}{\text{Ideology } (Ideologie)} \quad :: \quad \frac{\text{Foundations } (Basis)}{\text{Edifice } (Überbau)}$$

There is, as we can see, an *equality of shares* which, according
to Aristotle, make up an *analogy*. But the fact that there is an
analogical equality does not in any way imply that the terms in
the second pair can *truly* substitute for those in the first. They
can only substitute for them *metaphorically*. Every metaphor is
made up of such a transposition. If we say 'old age is to life as
evening is to the day', we articulate an analogy; but if we substitute the positions and say 'the evening of life' in order to
refer to old age, we articulate a metaphor. In the same way, if we
say 'the base or foundation of society', we enunciate a metaphor.
And the same is the case if we say *ideological superstructure or
edifice*.

We have now demonstrated the metaphorical character of
the term in question. Marx's oeuvre is outfitted with many
metaphors of this type, which possess an eminently literary

value – and, if you will, also a scientific one, seeing as these metaphors help illuminate his theories. Marx's theory is that the social relations of society govern and determine every ideological aspect of society, that is, the legal-political corpus, the state and the diverse set of social beliefs. His theory's metaphor is this: the economic base or foundation sustains the enormous ideological superstructure or edifice.

Let us do justice to Marx's literary style by respecting his metaphors as metaphors. And let us do justice to his scientific theories by not confusing them with their metaphorical aux-iliaries. A good many of the charges of 'determinism' and 'schematism' that bourgeois theorists level at Marx arise from these kinds of confusion, which are sadly propagated by Marx-ists themselves. It is Marxists, and not bourgeois ideologues, who have turned 'superstructure' into a scientific theory; what they have succeeded in doing is inverting Marx's theory and turning it into an ideology.

'Reflection' as Metaphor

In the fragment of the 1859 Preface we have analysed, Marx discreetly introduces a verbal dichotomy that can serve as a bridge between our discussion of the superstructure metaphor and the metaphor of 'reflection'. We have seen that in the terms of an analogy there are two pairs: the first of these, *Economic Structure/Ideology*, is the scientific expression of the theory, while the second, *Base/Edifice*, which has a linear correspondence with the first, is its metaphorical expression. This verbal dichotomy becomes even clearer if we remember the German terms employed by Marx: 'Economic Structure' is *ökonomische Struk-tur*, while 'edifice' or 'superstructure' is not *Superstruktur* but *Überbau*. It is symptomatic that in the scientific expression Marx uses *Struktur* – a Latin-derived word designating a *concrete epis-temological concept* that has an enormous theoretical importance in Marx's mature works, especially in *Capital*, as demonstrated by Maurice Godelier in his essay 'System, Structure and Contra-diction in *Capital*', which goes so far as to categorize Marx as a forerunner of contemporary structuralism.[43] And it is no less symptomatic that in the metaphorical expression Marx employs a German term, *Überbau*, which is not a scientific concept in itself but is rather its corresponding analogical term. Given that Marx, at the beginning of *Capital* and elsewhere, makes a point of spotting verbal dichotomies of this kind in the English authors of the seventeenth century – who tended to use a German-derived term, 'worth', for use-value, and a Latinate one, 'value', for exchange-value – what keeps us from making these same kinds of observations about Marx's own prose?

All of this makes us wary of the danger of thinking of Marxist theory in terms of 'superstructure', a word that forces us to imagine the world of ideology as superior and apart, as an independent realm floating above the social structure. The inverse is true: ideology lives and develops *in the social structure itself*: it is its interior continuation and plays, within it, an active everyday role. In accordance with an economic structure dominated by exploitation, ideology has until now justified this exploitation; it is also a form of exploitation itself, if one accepts the idea of *ideological surplus-value* which I have laid out in another book.[44] When Marcuse tells us that today 'the ideology comes to be embodied in the process of production itself',[45] all he is doing is correctly restating the Marxist theory of ideology as something not separate from, but immanent within, the social structure; something produced by that structure and active in its interior. When, for example, the state applies the legal ideology of private property to justify the accumulation of wealth in the hands of the few and its unequal distribution, is this not a case of ideology acting within and from the social structure? The fact that ideology is a product of the material situation in no way implies that

---

43   Maurice Godelier, 'Sistema, estructura y contradicción en "El capital"', in the multi-authored volume *Problemas del estructuralismo*, Siglo XXI, 1967, pp. 50ff.

44   Ludovico Silva, *La plusvalía ideológica*.

45   Herbert Marcuse, *One-Dimensional Man*, Routledge, 2006, p. 194.

it, ideology, is constituted in a world that lies 'above' the material situation: ideology remains tied to the social skeleton or, to use a metaphor of Althusser's, it acts as social 'cement'.[46]

Now, just as it has proven very popular to speak of 'ideological superstructure', it has proven no less popular to label the Marxist theory of ideology using the metaphor of 'ideological reflection'. Just as in the former case, this one involves a verbal dichotomy expressly deployed by Marx and completely upended by his interpreters. The latter have preferred to stick to the metaphor of ideology as a 'reflection' of the material structure of society and, in the process, have missed the scientific terms with which Marx develops the problem, centred on the word *Ausdruck* or 'expression', which defines ideology as the *expression* of material relations.

The book of mine that I have mentioned above, *Ideological Surplus-Value*, contains a detailed discussion of this point.[47] I will repeat it here, with a special emphasis on a new set of observations as well as on the problem's literary dimension, with the goal of highlighting how a careful reading of Marx's style can not only help us to define it as a style but also help us better understand the real theoretical content of his writings.

The reflection metaphor is expressed in a classic passage from *The German Ideology*:

If in all ideology men and their relations appear upside-down as in a *camera obscura*, this phenomenon arises just as much from their historical life-process as the inversion of objects on the retina does from their physical life-process. In direct contrast to German philosophy which descends from heaven to earth, here it is a matter of ascending from earth to heaven. That is to say, not of setting out from what men say, imagine,

46   Cf. Louis Althusser, 'Note on the ISAs', in *On the Reproduction of Capitalism: Ideology and Ideological State Apparatuses*, Verso, 2014, p. 227.

47   See Silva, *La plusvalía ideológica*, chapter 2.

conceive, nor from men as narrated, thought of, imagined, conceived, in order to arrive at men in the flesh; but setting out from real, active men, and on the basis of their real life-process demonstrating the development of the ideological reflexes and echoes [*der ideologischen Reflexe und Echos*] of this life-process. The phantoms [*Nebelbildungen*, 'nebulous pictures'] formed in the brains of men are also, necessarily, sublimates of their material life-process, which is empirically verifiable and bound to material premises. Morality, religion, metaphysics, and all the rest of ideology as well as the forms of consciousness corresponding to these, thus no longer retain the semblance of independence. They have no history, no development; but men, developing their material production and their material intercourse, alter, along with this their actual world, also their thinking and the products of their thinking.[48]

After *The German Ideology*, Marx abandons his 'reflection' metaphor almost completely; it only appears in his writings on very few occasions. The same is not true of the co-author of *The German Ideology*, Engels. The author of *Anti-Dühring* insisted on the metaphor many times, especially in his late texts, and gave it many variations including 'religious reflection', 'legal reflection', 'aesthetic reflection' and so on. He also never bothered much about differentiating between metaphor and theory. His mistake did not lie in his use of the metaphor – there is nothing wrong, after all, with an appropriate and pertinent metaphor – but in not having published *The German Ideology*, a work that on its own would have settled the many distortions that the Marx-Engels theory of ideology suffered during Engels's lifetime and that we will discuss later. For now, let us analyse the text quoted above.

As with 'superstructure', here we encounter an analogy in the strict sense. Better yet, we encounter two entwined, complementary analogies. The first of these, which serves as the base for the second, can be represented like this:

---

48   Marx and Engels, 'The German Ideology', pp. 36–7.

Ideology		Reflection
Human Mind	::	Camera Obscura

Put another way, ideology appears in the human mind in the same way that an optical reflection appears in a camera obscura. Just as an inverted reflection of physical reality appears in a camera obscura, an inverted representation of the world (that is, a vision of the world in which ideas drive men instead of men driving ideas) appears in the human mind. Such is the analogy. The metaphor appears when the terms are substituted, that is, when we speak of 'ideological reflection'. This is not the only metaphor that could arise out of this process: one could speak of a 'photographic mind', of 'mental reflection' or – why not? – of 'ideological photography'. All of these are just as legitimate as 'ideological reflection'. Another side of the issue is that this metaphor is typical of the age that invented photography.[49] After the invention of electricity, too, every poet spoke of his 'electrifying' lover, a figure that lives on in various languages as a kind of residual metaphor which has lost its original brightness and become commonplace. The reflection metaphor has also become a cliché, that is, it has undergone a process of reification or hardening.

The second analogy detaches itself from the first and affords us with more specific analytical material. This is its form in diagram:

Ideology		Typical Reflection
Historico-Natural Reality	::	Physico-Natural Reality

49 Leonardo da Vinci had already conceived of the camera obscura; the first photograph is from 1826 and a further perfection of the process takes place in 1838. Marx and Engels write *The German Ideology* in 1845–6.

That is: a society's ideology bears the same relationship to its history and its material life-process as the image produced on the retina does to its immediate physical reality. 'The inversion of objects on the retina' – Marx tells us – 'arises from the physical life-process.' In the same way, the inverted representation of the world (that is, the *ideological* belief that ideas produce history and not history ideas) that makes up ideology responds to the historical and material life-processes of societies and men. In the first case, physical reality determines the reflection; in the second, historical reality determines ideology. The analogy gets us this far. The metaphor once again appears through a substitution of terms: to speak of *ideological reflection*, as Marx tells us, is to engage in metaphor.

We must make a firm distinction between metaphorical expressions and theoretico-explanatory expressions. But first, the reader should meditate on the following: Marx speaks to us of 'ideological reflexes and *echoes*'. There is, then, more than one metaphor. Along with the plastic metaphor, he hands us an acoustic one: ideology is like an echo of real social life. This acoustic metaphor is not carefully developed like the other one; nevertheless, 'ideological echo' has just as much metaphorical power and legitimacy within the text as 'ideological reflection'. If Marx and Engels had highlighted 'echo' more than 'reflection', there is no doubt that what passes today for 'reflection theory' in so many Marxist works would be an 'echo theory'. Morals, metaphysics, religion, legal forms: all would be categorized as society's *ideological echoes*. Marxist histories of philosophy would not tell us that Plato's philosophy is an 'ideological reflection' of an aristocratic slave-owning society; they would tell us that such a philosophy is an *ideological echo* of that society. None of which would be all that serious if these expressions were used metaphorically – at best, we might ask for a bit more literary originality to replace the liturgical repetition of Marx's metaphors – but what is serious, what is, in fact, disastrous for contemporary Marxism, is that metaphors like these are presented as scientific theories, as complete explanations of 'historical materialism'. It is impressive, for instance, how many theoretical crudities appear in treatises and manuals on 'aesthetic reflection'. And we are not just speaking of the inescapable manuals: the most authoritative and profound scholars of Marx commit this same error. We will cite two names at random. First, let us remember the conspicuous English Marxist George Thomson. In his work *First Philosophers*, he says of a certain phrase from Heraclitus ('All things are an exchange for fire, and fire for all things, as goods for gold and gold for goods') that it is nothing more than 'an *ideological reflection* of an economy based on the production of commodities'.[50] And Lukács, in his *Prolegomena to a Marxist Aesthetics*, tells us that 'at the foundation of this book is the general idea that scientific reflection [!] and aesthetic reflection reflect the same objective reality'.[51] If one hopes to create a Marxist science of ideology, why return repeatedly to Marx's metaphors instead of to his scientific explanations?

Once again: the problem is not the metaphors themselves but, rather, their relation to theory. To say of Heraclitus's phrase that it is the ideological reflection of the production of commodities is to say something that is metaphorically correct, but it is not at all the same as scientifically explaining the historical and social origin of a thought that takes gold as the universal equivalent and confronts it with all other commodities. One would have to explain how the evolution of the monetary system is expressed in Heraclitus's phrase, and that is not accomplished simply by saying that the phrase is the 'ideological reflection' of the production of commodities. The same holds for Lukács's words: neither science nor art truly 'reflects' anything – would it not be better to say instead that science and art *express* a reality which is the same, and that each of them does so with an *active*

50   George Thomson, *The First Philosophers*, Lawrence & Wishart, 1972, p. 301.

51   György Lukács, *Prolegómenos a una estética marxista*, Grijalbo, 1965, p. 12.

language rather than as *passive reflections*? If we follow the reflection metaphor strictly, we would have to conclude that science and art *photograph* reality. Would Lukács be willing to accept this as a scientific explanation of Marxist gnoseology?

All of this will become clearer if we return to our analysis of the analogy put forth in *The German Ideology*. The relationship between ideology and historical reality is a relationship of dependence, comparable to the relationship of dependence between optical reflection and physico-natural reality. There are two ways to take this comparison: 1) as an analogy, the source of metaphors such as 'ideological reflection'; 2) as a scientific explanation.

If we *take it as an analogy*, we accept that it does not constitute a complete scientific explanation but, rather, a literary illustration of a theory. This can only be demonstrated if we have previously demonstrated that the expressions in question do not constitute a scientific explanation.

Where, in effect, are we led if we *take it as a scientific explanation*? To give a preview of our conclusion, we will represent Marx's theory just as bourgeois ideologues do: as an absurd, mechanistic determinism, if not a unilateral causalism.

Let us illustrate the explanation with a diagram:

Ideology

↕

(A)

Historical Reality

Optical Reflection

↑

(B)

Physico-Natural Reality

The question is whether, *effectively* (not just in the world of metaphor), the *relationship* between the terms in (A) is *the same* as that between the terms in (B). The different arrows seek to show that *truly and effectively, the relationship is not the same.* What is the relationship between the terms in (B)? The relationship between physico-natural reality and optical reflection is *causal*; physical reality *causally determines* (or, put less formally, 'produces') the optical reflection. A determination is *causal* when, as Bunge shows us, it is the 'determination of the effect by the efficient (external) cause'.[52] On top of that, in the case of optical reflection we are dealing with an *irreversible* determination that goes from reality to the eye. Now, is this the same type of determination that exists between historical reality and ideology according to Marxist theory? Absolutely not. Historical reality *does not causally determine* ideological formations. In the first place, this is because history can externally determine individuals, but it can also do so internally, from within these same individuals, something attested to today by disciplines like the sociology of knowledge and, more appropriately, psychoanalysis, when they locate *social* determinations in the unconscious or preconscious of the individual (determinations which are nothing but *ideology*). In the second place, because determination is *reversible* and *multivocal* here – if it is, in effect, historical and social reality (the 'material life-process') which gives a society's ideology its character – it is equally true that once this character (↑) impinges on social reality, it acts on this reality (↓) and, in sum, ideologically determines it. We should not perceive a vicious cycle in this reversibility: it is empirically necessary to examine the material conditions of a society *in order to* understand the true character – which is an *a posteriori* character – of that society's ideology. A vicious cycle would exist if things were reversed, that is, if one could find out a society's material character by merely analysing its

---

52 Mario Bunge, *Causality and Modern Science*, Transaction Publishers, 2009, p. 18.

ideology. This cannot be done, precisely because every ideology is a *justification* of an order and a set of material interests that *pre-exist* it. Historically speaking, it is only with the full development of capitalism in the twentieth century that a full capitalist ideology has been able to constitute itself, an ideology that justifies the totality of the system in each of its parts – something made possible by the advances in the means of mass communication. And finally, historical reality determines ideology *multivocally*, and ideology, in turn, multivocally overdetermines historical reality. In effect, the general character of a society's ideology is determined by the different facets of its material apparatus – the regime of private property, the monetary and mercantile economy, the social division of labour, the class struggle. Looked at another way, this ideology multivocally influences the material apparatus when it responds to its determinations through legal bodies, social institutions like 'free enterprise', a Christian morality that authorizes and recommends material poverty, the genre of social science that, divided into different 'compartments', reproduces the material division of labour on the theoretical level and so on. If private property is an *alienation* in the material order, legal ideology will take it upon itself to prove that private property is an 'inalienable' right. If an underdeveloped country is economically dependent on an imperial power, both the imperial power and the underdeveloped country will disseminate the ideology of 'nationalism' and 'self-determination'. This is a real game in which a material reality produces an ideology that *denies* the true character of this material reality by idealizing it. The ideology then actively influences this reality and so negates it doubly, that is, it *affirms* it. This is why the essence of every ideology is the profound and constant affirmation of the existing material order; it is its supreme justification.

By now, we have demonstrated the inadequacy of the two sets of terms that made up the initial analogy; that is, we have demonstrated their scientific inadequacy. What we have not done is demonstrated their metaphorical inadequacy.

What is most curious is that if Marx had stuck to the original metaphorical formulation of his thesis, there would be no reason – at least no formal reason – for the confusion we have discussed and that has entrapped so many Marxists. But what is certain, what can be confirmed objectively, is that Marx used the metaphor of 'reflection' very few times. Instead, on innumerable occasions he spoke of ideology as the *expression* (*Ausdruck*) of material relations. This does constitute an opening for scientific analysis because to say that ideology is expression is the same as to describe it as *language*, that is, as action rather than passion, as an active element and not as a mere passive reflection.

The current media, the very marrow of capitalist ideology – are they passive reflections of society or are they rather a relentless language that imposes itself on us daily and that penetrates to those 'mnemonics' of which Freud spoke? What is jurisprudence if not a convoluted language for the purpose of justifying the existing social order? What is religion, if not the subtle manipulation of ethical symbols? What is speculative philosophy, if not a language that has by now been torn apart, analysed and critiqued by scientific philosophy? Ideology is the expression of society – it is its language. Language and consciousness, Marx tells us, are *gesellschaftliche Produkte*. And his theory of ideology is scientifically formulated when, instead of speaking of 'reflection', he speaks in this way: 'The ruling ideas are nothing more than the ideal expression [*Ausdruck*] of the dominant material relationships, the dominant material relationships grasped as ideas.'[53]

All of this shows us why contemporary Marxism needs to review its 'readings' of Marx's works and why it needs to see his oeuvre from a *stylistic* point of view. The careful examination of style is, after all, the primordial method for distinguishing what is metaphor, wordplay, illustration or ornament from what is properly theoretical in a given style. Such a study of Marx's oeuvre is all the more important. Marx belongs to a class of

---

53   Marx and Engels, 'The German Ideology', p. 59.

scientific writers who are very rare today. His determination to overcome every division of labour in his own person led him to tackle every aspect of scientific labour, beginning with the literary aspect. Why do we insist on denying Marx something that always preoccupied him – his literary style?

Marx tells us that, in communist society, 'man appropriates his integral essence in an integral way, as a total man'.[54] Syntactically formulated, this is the path to overcoming the alienation produced by the division of labour. Man today is, as Marcuse has described him: *one-dimensional*, unilateral. Among scientific researchers in contemporary American universities, it is common to complete a rough draft of a text and then hand it over to a 'stylist' who can produce a polished version. Marx would have rejected such a division of labour in horror.

So, given that he was an omnidimensional, omnilateral scientist, who devoted as much care to his calculations as to the precision of his metaphors, why denigrate and divide him? Why take his metaphors for what they are not? This is a comparable, if inverse, error to that committed by bourgeois, one-dimensional scientists who, irritated by Marx's metaphors, insist that his whole oeuvre is a metaphor, and that the theory of surplus-value is the product of a feverish, messianic imagination.

Religion as Metaphor

We have seen that, strictly speaking, both 'superstructure' and 'reflection' are metaphors and that Marx – who possessed an impressive mastery of the art of metaphor from a very young age – used them as such. Both terms are literary illustrations of a scientific theory: the theory of ideology, which is intimately connected to Marx's general materialist theory. That so many

---

54   Marx, 'Economic and Philosophical Manuscripts (1844)', p. 351. [*Trans.*: Silva's translation of *allseitige* is 'omnilateral'. The standard English rendering is 'integral'. The German reads: 'Der Mensch eignet sich sein allseitiges Wesen auf eine allseitige Art an, also als ein totaler Mensch.']

commentators of both yesterday and today speak of a supposed 'reflection theory' and of a 'superstructure theory' is nothing but a sign of intellectual laziness; after all, it is much easier and more comfortable to avoid scientific explanations and to stick to their metaphorical substitutes. This is one of the reasons for the notorious 'schematicism' of the manuals.

The metaphor of religion, to which Marx returned time and again across all of his phases, has been somewhat more fortunate than those we have studied so far. It has not been the victim of too many mystifications, perhaps because it is a metaphor specifically meant to destroy that mystification par excellence – religion.

As a general definition of this metaphor, we could say that its concrete mission in Marx's work was to provide an analogy that would illuminate – by way of comparison to religious alienation – the phenomenon of the alienation of labour and the phenomenon of historical and social alienation in general. This is how we find it in the *1844 Manuscripts* and so it remains in major works such as the *Grundrisse*, *Capital* and *Theories of Surplus Value*. In the *Manuscripts*, as we have seen, it goes as follows: 'Just as in religion the spontaneous activity of the human imagination, the human brain and the human heart detaches itself from the individual and reappears as the alien activity of a god or of a devil, so the activity of the worker is not his own spontaneous activity. It belongs to another, it is a loss of his self.'[55] This is a perfect analogy: A:B :: C:D, that is: *the same relationship* obtains between the mental activity of religion and the mind itself on the one hand, and between the productive activity of the worker and the worker himself on the other. This relationship is one of *alienation*.

As articulated in the *1844 Manuscripts*, the first form of this alienation did not involve productive activity itself but the alienation of the *product* of labour. In a sentence from *Capital* that

---

55 Marx, 'Economic and Philosophical Manuscripts (1844)', pp. 326–7.

has been cited a thousand times, we read that just as in religion the products of the human mind turn against man, so in the regime of the production of commodities the products of man's own hands turn against him. In the equally famous chapter on commodity fetishism, Marx expressly presents his metaphor *as an analogy*:

> The commodity form, and the value-relation of the products of labour within which it appears, have absolutely no connection with the physical nature of the commodity and the material [*dinglich*] relations arising out of this. It is nothing but the definite social relation between men themselves which assumes here, for them, the fantastic form of a relation between things. In order, therefore, to find an analogy [*eine Analogie*] we must take flight into the misty realm of religion. There the products of the human brain appear as autonomous figures endowed with a life of their own, which enter into relations both with each other and with the human race. So it is in the world of commodities with the products of men's hands. I call this the fetishism.[56]

'Alienation' and 'fetishism' are not the same thing: while every instance of commodity fetishism involves alienation, not every form of alienation involves commodity fetishism. Here, however, we are dealing with what Marx in 1844 called the 'alienation of the product'. Is it not significant that, in order to describe it, he uses the exact same analogy in 1867 as he did in 1844? The analogy now looks like this: the relationship between the religious products of the mind and the mind itself *is the same as the relationship* between the commodity products of man and man himself. The 'equal shares' that make up the analogy are nothing more than the alienation that exists in both cases. It is as if we said: 4:2 :: 6:3. The arithmetical relation is the same. Religious alienation serves as a perfect metaphor for the alienation of labour.

---

56   Marx, *Capital, Volume 1*, p. 165.

Another way of using religion as metaphor arises in the *1844 Manuscripts* and the *Grundrisse* when Marx establishes a curious comparison between Christ and money.

In a set of reading notes from 1844, we find money defined as an *alienated mediator*: what is alienated is the *mediating activity* itself (a precursor of 'commodity fetishism', in which money appears as the ultimate form of alienation). Money, which is nothing but a social relation, seems to become a *material thing* possessing mediating powers over the relations between people and leading them to become things insofar as money becomes personified. 'Man becomes poorer as man' – that is, separated from this mediator – 'the richer this mediator becomes.' (This formula is repeated in *Capital* and in *Theories of Surplus Value* as *Personifizierung der Sache und Versachlichung der Person*, that is, the personification of the thing and the thingification of the person.) Now:

> Christ originally represents (1) man before God, (2) God for man and (3) man for man. In the same way *money* originally represents (1) private property for private property; (2) society for private property; (3) private property for society. But Christ is God *alienated* and *man* alienated. God continues to have value only in so far as he represents Christ, man continues to have value only in so far as he represents Christ. Likewise with money.[57]

Following this analogy, we find that man only has value in this society insofar as he represents money. Marx measures the *value* of commodities according to the labour *time* that is socially necessary for their production – what would he say of the contemporary phrase 'time is money'? The comparison with Christ is even stronger insofar as Christ has always been represented as the spirit of material poverty. It is more curious,

---

57 Marx, 'Excerpts from James Mill's *Elements of Political Economy*', in *Early Writings*, p. 261.

however, if we remember an ancient tradition, expressed in Augustine, that gave Christ the name *Mediator*. Saint Augustine writes in his *Tractates on the Gospel of John* that Christ was *homo manifestus, Deus occultus* and that therefore: *Unus enim Deus, et unus mediator Dei et hominum homo Christus Iesus*.[58] Christ's dual nature – man on the outside and God inside – inspires the metaphor of money, which is use-value on the outside and exchange-value on the inside. And, just as Christ the man is alienated into omnipotent God, so in man money is alienated into an omnipotent thing.

The same Christ–money metaphor is found in the *Grundrisse*, where it is expressed even more appropriately as far as the economic analysis is concerned. After speaking of the importance of the concept of capital in the modern economy, Marx writes:

> It is important to note that wealth as such, i.e. bourgeois wealth, is always expressed to the highest power as exchange value, where it is posited as *mediator*, as the mediation of the extremes of exchange value and use value themselves. This intermediary situation [*Mitte*] always appears as the *economic* relation in its completeness, because it comprises the opposed poles, and ultimately always appears as a one-sidedly higher power *vis-à-vis* the extremes themselves; because the movement, or the relation, which *originally* appears as mediatory between the extremes necessarily develops dialectically to where it appears as mediation with itself, as the subject [*Subjekt*] for whom the extremes are merely its moments, whose autonomous presupposition it suspends in order to posit itself, through their suspension, as that which alone is autonomous. Thus, in the religious sphere, Christ, the

---

58 'For there us one God, and one Mediator between God and men, the man Christ Jesus.' Saint Augustine, 'Tractate LXVI from *Homilies on the Gospel of John*', in *Nicene and Post-Nicene Fathers of the Christian Church*, Vol. 7, ed. Philip Schaff, trans. John Gibb, Christian Literature Publishing Company, 1888.

mediator between God and humanity – a mere instrument of circulation between the two – becomes their unity, God-man, and, as such, becomes more important than God; the saints more important than Christ; the popes more important than the saints.[59]

In this fragment, the metaphor is further stylized and refined in a way that reflects how Marx has perfected his economic analysis, which was still insufficient in the *1844 Manuscripts*. The initial Christ–money metaphor is now the more subtle Christ–exchange-value metaphor. Both possess a double value: Christ is not just God, he is man, and exchange-value is both itself and a use-value that *incarnates* it, the same way that God is *incarnate* in man. And, just as in the God-man unity the first member or 'God' becomes the mediation between God and man, that is, his own mediation, so too in the use-value-exchange-value unity, this last term strangely arises as the mediator between use and exchange, that is, as its own mediator. And so, Christ, as mediator, becomes even more important than God, who, after all, lives in celestial solitude. In the same way, exchange-value, as mediator, becomes more important than use-value. This is a metaphorical representation of an entire economy based on exchange-value, in which the market is more important than man, in which production serves the needs of the market rather than the needs of man, just as religion attends more to the administrative needs of the Church than to the needs of God. And, just as the economy is founded on the competition of all against all and not on distribution according to need, so religion is based on the fear of hell rather than on the love of heaven.

The religion metaphor, or religion as metaphor, also appears in *Theories of Surplus Value*, Volume 4 of *Capital*, which was written between 1861 and 1863, as well as in other manuscripts from 1863–5. Its form of appearance resembles what we have

---

59   Karl Marx, *Grundrisse: Foundations of the Critique of Political Economy (Rough Draft)*, trans. Martin Nicolaus, Penguin, 1993, pp. 331–2.

already seen in the *1844 Manuscripts* and *Capital* as it involves the alienation of the product and how the product dominates the producer. (Contrary to authors such as Althusser and Bottigelli, who claim that 'alienation' disappears in the mature Marx, these manuscripts present incontrovertible proof: the word *Entfremdung* appears many times, as does a now perfectly *mature*, de-Hegelianized theory of alienation.)

In a partially preserved manuscript from 1863–5, Marx writes:

> The capitalist functions only as *personified* capital, capital as a person, just as the worker is no more than *labour* person-ified. That labour is for him just effort and torment, whereas it belongs to the capitalist as a substance that creates and increases wealth, and in fact it is an element of capital, incor-porated into it in the production process as its living, variable component. Hence the rule of the capitalist over the worker is the rule of things over man, of dead labour over the living, of the product over the producer. For the commodities that become the instruments of rule over the workers (merely as the instruments of the rule of *capital* itself) are mere conse-quences of the process of production; they are its products. Thus at the level of material production, of the life process in the realm of the social – for that is what the process of production is – we find the *same* situation that we find in *religion* at the ideological level, namely the inversion of subject into object and *vice versa* . . . What we are confronted by here is the *alienation* [*Entfremdung*] of man from his own labour. To that extent the worker stands on a higher plane than the capitalist from the outset, since the latter has his roots in the process of alienation and finds absolute satisfac-tion in it whereas right from the start the worker is a victim who confronts it as a rebel and experiences it as a process of enslavement.[60]

---

60   Marx, 'Results of the Immediate Process of Production', in *Capital, Volume 1*, pp. 989–90.

This is not the place to highlight the full theoretical significance of a passage so important to Marx's understanding of alienation. We can, however, affirm that this is a text that is both much more explicit than any from 1844 as well as one integrated into an already perfected economic analysis that draws on categories that do not exist in the *Manuscripts*: surplus-value, the concept of 'labour-power' and so on. Nevertheless, just as in 1844, it contains the metaphor of religion, something that constitutes a real stylistic constant in Marx's handling of the problem of alienation. From his youthful Feuerbachian phase, Marx had learned that religious alienation consists of – to put it briefly – the conversion of subject into object, of the true creator (man) into the created being or creature, from which arises the domination of the creator by the creation and therefore of the subject by the object. This would always serve him as a great metaphor for describing economic alienation, in which the products of man, commodities, become the governing agents of social life – become the true social beings – insofar as men pack themselves in and become helpless, passive, submissive things. It is the dominion of materialized, objectified, dead labour over living labour. As he writes in a preface to Volume 1 of *Capital*: 'We suffer not only from the living, but from the dead. *Le mort saisit le vif!*'[61]

Other Features: The Concrete Spirit, the Polemical Spirit, the Spirit of Mockery

So far, I have defined Marx's style in terms of an architectonic style, a dialectical style and a style that employs great metaphors like that of religion. Before a final appraisal, I shall briefly note other features that, without being minor, do not require detailed explanations. I call these Marx's *concrete spirit*, his *polemical spirit* and his *spirit of mockery*.

---

61   Marx, *Capital, Volume 1*, p. 91.

What I call the *concrete spirit* of Marx's literary and intellectual style is precisely the coexistence, in his writing, of a notable capacity for abstraction paired with – and *dominated by* – an equally remarkable capacity for concretion. Althusser was right when, in an article from his *For Marx*, he characterized 'the personal style of Marx's experience' as his 'extraordinary sensitivity to the concrete which gave such force of conviction and revelation to each of his encounters with reality'.[62] In effect, Marx's true object of study was concrete history, that 'concrete totality' of which he spoke in the General Introduction to his *Economy*, written along with the *Grundrisse* and later substituted by the Preface to the *Contribution to the Critique of Political Economy*. In this General Introduction, he articulates his famous methodological principle: 'The concrete is concrete because it is the concentration of many determinations, hence unity of the diverse.'[63] However, in the same text, he explains that the concrete element in thought always arises as a result, a result that is arrived at through abstraction. This is the path taken by Volume 1 of *Capital*, which goes from the abstract to the concrete, from the commodity in its most general form to its concrete form in money, from fetishism in its most abstract form to the concrete process of the production of surplus-value, where fetishism is created in that 'hidden abode of production'. This methodological principle, which sums up an entire deductive-inductive movement in the concept of totality – which goes from abstract to concrete and concrete to abstract – also serves as a stylistic principle: Marx's style, especially in that artistic whole which is Volume 1 of *Capital*, presents itself as a constant intellectual movement that goes from abstract to concrete and vice versa, something conspicuously evident in the vocabulary he uses. Thus, for example, in the first few chapters, which constitute a moment of maximum abstraction of economic categories and a purely synchronic analysis, the predominant word is *form*: the

---

62 Louis Althusser, *For Marx*, Verso, 2006, p. 82.
63 Marx, *Grundrisse*, p. 101.

commodity *form*, which unfolds in the *forms* of value, exchange-value and use-value; the *form* of exchange-value, based on the *form* of equivalence and so on. The commodity is the 'elemental *form*' (or 'economic cell'); labour causes 'matter to change *form*'; *value* appears in the linen and the coat 'only in so far as abstraction is made from their special qualities, only in so far as both possess the same *quality* of being *human labour*' which acquires the *form* of 'abstract human labour'; commodity fetishism makes these appear – given their *double form* – as 'physically metaphysical' beings. *Et cetera!*[64]

But having crossed this abstract threshold (which earned Marx the label of 'metaphysician' during his life . . .), Marx's style adapts itself to the new methodological phase that must occupy itself with concrete phenomena such as the division of labour in manufacture and machinery and large-scale industry. Thus, in speaking of the division of labour, Marx's style penetrates to the last interstices of this phenomenon by employing examples and metaphors, some of them quite curious, like the one about the businessman who hoped to make each worker complete a different task with each hand and who is doomed to fail until he finds 'two-headed men'. In speaking of machinery, he begins with the definition of machinery itself (the abstract moment) and later, through an analysis of the simplest of machines (starting with the water-wheel), he arrives at a most complete description of modern machinery. This descriptive process, which could have been an invitation to fall into erudite pedantry and verbal tedium, actually allows Marx to enrich his descriptions with brilliant comparisons and – most importantly, of course – to continuously slip *theory* into his empirical descriptions.

Despite his enormous capacity for abstraction, Marx never fell into speculative glibness: he did not conceive of capitalism by 'thinking' but instead by studying specific, concrete phenomena.

---

64   All of these expressions appear in the first chapter of Marx, *Capital, Volume 1*.

This effort translated marvellously to his style, which – as is only appropriate for a scientific writer – is the style of a writer with a great capacity for flight who never loses sight of the ground. 'Every profound philosophical problem', he wrote in *The German Ideology*, 'is resolved quite simply into an empirical fact.'[65]

The other two features of Marx's style which we have identified – his *polemical spirit* and his *spirit of mockery* – are, in reality, a single characteristic, a single facet. The distinction involves nothing more than the nuances taken on by this facet.

As Maximilien Rubel has pointed out in his *Karl Marx: Essai de biographie intellectuelle*,[66] what prompted Marx to study economics was his indignant observation of poverty among workers; that ethical and political indignation that gives his works a tone of frank denunciation, a tone which would never disappear from his style, even when it became more coldly scientific. This is why it has been claimed that Marx's scientific work is nothing more than a redemptive, messianic ideology, though those who claim this ignore, for one thing, that Marx was the greatest decrier of ideology (in the name of theory, science and class consciousness) and, for another, they confuse the duty of science with a supposed 'value neutrality' (Max Weber, Karl Mannheim). They think that science should restrict itself to *enunciations*, and that *denunciations* should be left to politicians. What they achieve by this is, in the end, nothing more than a subtle new apology for the division of labour. They also reveal the surprise and irritation that a social scientist like Marx inspires in them – after all, such a division does not exist in his labour, which formed a harmonious whole in which his objective enunciations and no-less-objective denunciations, clad as they are in an ethical musculature, always interlock.

---

65   Marx and Engels, 'The German Ideology', p. 39.
66   Maximilien Rubel, *Karl Marx: Essai de biographie intellectuelle*, Librairie Rivière, 1957, Part 1, chapter 5.

This indignation birthed Marx's *polemical spirit*, the critical disposition that always characterized him as a writer. Very few scientists can be counted among those who intimately combine the spirit of science and the spirit of polemic and critique.

Marx produced philosophical, political, economic, sociological and even literary criticism (let us not forget his critique, in *The Holy Family*, of Eugène Sue's *The Mysteries of Paris*, or his many stray observations on literature). His acid political criticism was so corrosive that it forced him to dance his way across Europe, exiled by one government after another. His philosophical criticism is revealed, above all, in *The German Ideology*, in which he exposed the ideological and mystifying character of philosophy up to that point, and went so far as to call for the future extinction of philosophy and to cruelly stigmatize philosophers by claiming that 'philosophy and the study of the actual world have the same relation to one another as onanism and sexual love'.[67] His economic criticism encompasses all of his work from 1844 on, and is truly impressive in its vastness – there is practically no important modern social scientist whom he did not touch upon. An exceptional testament to this formidable critical apparatus is his *Theories of Surplus Value*, a prodigious manuscript consisting of thousands of pages (Dietz's edition takes up three volumes), in which he critically surveys all vulgar and classical economic theory. A history of philosophy, for example, that fulfilled the same criteria as this history of political economy would be forced to upend the highly 'harmonious' history of philosophy that has been institutionalized since Hegel.

Some of the most personal stylistic features of Marx's writing were nourished during all of this critical labour and in the very practice of this labour. His polemical capability is proverbial, and it is coupled with a style that made his attacks hit even harder. All that is needed to fully demonstrate this is his *Poverty of Philosophy* or 'Anti-Proudhon', which is an excellent model of

---

67   Marx and Engels, 'The German Ideology', p. 236.

polemical literature. There has never been such a fierce and relentless evisceration as that conducted by Marx on Proudhon. And it was all the harsher given that they had been friends in Paris just a short time before.

It is a critique so harsh that it occasionally reads as over the top.

And it is Marx's stylistic virtuosity that contributes to the harshness of the critique: he takes a number of quotations from Proudhon's *Philosophie de la misère* and analyses them down to the last detail, highlighting their 'hidden messages', the spirit of their words, the ideology behind the ostensible theory, the belief beneath the science, the metaphysical presupposition behind the theoretical supposition. The first foreword is telling:

> M. Proudhon has the misfortune of being peculiarly misunderstood in Europe. In France, he has the right to be a bad economist, because he is reputed to be a good German philosopher. In Germany, he has the right to be a bad philosopher, because he is reputed to be one of the ablest French economists. Being both German and economist at the same time, we desire to protest against this double error.[68]

We should note, in passing, that this is a magnificent example of the dialectical style we described above. In order to decipher 'Proudhon's mysteries', Marx tells us, one would have to become English and speak of economy, only to discover that one would have to become German and speak of 'the metaphysics of the economy'. This is the case because, 'If the Englishman

---

68   Marx, 'The Poverty of Philosophy', p. 109. 'M. Proudhon a le malheur d'être singulièrement méconnu en Europe. En France, il a le droit d'être mauvais économiste, parce qu'il passe pour être bon philosophe allemand. En Allemagne, il a le droit d'être mauvais philosophe, parce qu'il passe pour être économiste français des plus forts. Nous, en notre qualité d'Allemand et d'économiste à la fois, nous avons voulu protester contre cette double erreur.'

transforms men into hats, the German transforms hats into ideas.'[69] Proudhon is a 'quasi-Hegel', so Marx decides it is fitting to give him lessons in Hegelianism, but lessons conducted in a spirit of mockery. The exposition of Hegelian ideas Marx gives, caught as it is between the humorous and the transcendent, is remarkable:

> The yes becoming no, the no becoming yes, the yes becoming both yes and no, the no becoming both no and yes, the contraries balance, neutralise, paralyse each other . . . Apply this method to the categories of political economy, and you have the logic and metaphysics of political economy, or, in other words, you have the economic categories that everybody knows translated into a little-known language which makes them look as if they had newly blossomed forth in an intellect of pure reason.[70]

As we can see, he moves from the critical to the polemical style and from there to a style of mockery – here is the entire stylistic gamut of this aspect of Marx. Along with Proudhon, Marx stigmatized numerous authors throughout his works with stray missives. It is curious to note that – perhaps in memory of his Proudhonian experience – he launched many of these attacks in French, as when he characterizes Destutt de Tracy in Volume 2 of *Capital* by saying that he represents 'le crétinisme bourgeois

---

69   Marx, 'The Poverty of Philosophy', p. 161. 'Si l'Anglais transforme les hommes en chapeaux, l'Allemand transforme les chapeaux en idées.'

70   Marx, 'The Poverty of Philosophy', pp. 164–5. 'Le oui devenant non, le non devenant oui, le oui devenant à la fois oui et non, le non devenant à la fois non et oui, les contraires se balancent, se neutralisent, se paralysent . . . Appliquez cette méthode aux catégories de l'économie politique, et vous aurez la logique et la métaphysique de l'économie politique, ou, en d'autres termes, vous aurez les catégories économiques connues de tout le monde, traduites dans un langage peu connu, qui leur donne l'air d'être fraîchement écloses dans une tête raison pure.'

dans toute sa béatitude'.[71] On more than one occasion he reserved a special fury for those 'petulant and cranky epigones': the academics of the German universities. He also brutally attacked numerous intellectual fetishes as if they were people. One of these, 'culture', he writes, is based on 'the antithesis between poverty and wealth, between poverty and luxury, because, to the extent that a smaller quantity of labour suffices to produce the necessary means of subsistence, part of the labour becomes more and more superfluous and can therefore be used in the production of luxury articles'.[72] And of the abstraction that is the 'commodity', he writes what we have elsewhere described as a prophecy of television: 'But as soon as it emerges as a commodity, it changes into a thing which transcends sensuousness. It not only stands with its feet on the ground, but, in relation to all other commodities, it stands on its head, and evolves out of its wooden brain grotesque ideas, far more wonderful than if it were to begin dancing of its own free will.'[73]

Every reader of Marx will easily remember hundreds of instances in which he demonstrates a notable verbal virtuosity in attack, in polemic and in the ruthless mockery of both thing-ified personages and personified things. He did not even spare himself. Not only did he criticize his own errors, he even waxed ironic about his own life and misfortunes. A vivid testimony to this is his correspondence with Engels. With a certain humor-ous melancholy, while he was writing *Capital* he wrote to his

---

71   Karl Marx, *Capital, Volume 2*, trans. David Fernbach, Penguin, 1993, p. 564: 'bourgeois idiocy in all its beatitude'.

72   Karl Marx, *Theories of Surplus Value: Part 1*, Lawrence and Wishart, 1969, p. 306.

73   Marx, *Capital, Volume 1*, pp. 163–4. 'Aber sobald er als Ware auftritt, verwandelt er sich in ein sinnlich übersinnliches Ding. Er steht nicht nur mit seinen Füßen auf dem Boden, sondern er stellt sich allen andren Waren gegenüber auf den Kopf und entwickelt aus seinem Holzkopf Grillen, viel wunderlicher, als wenn er aus freien Stücken zu tanzen begänne.'

friend that never had money been written about . . . by someone with so little of it! And in another letter, apropos the 'pest of carbuncles', which did not allow him to finish his 'damned book', he writes to Engels: 'I trust that the bourgeoisie will remember my carbuncles until their dying day.'[74]

---

74 'Marx to Engels, 22 June 1867', in *Karl Marx and Friedrich Engels Collected Works*, Vol. 42, p. 383.

3

A Stylistic Appraisal of Marx's Oeuvre

The expression of an architectonic vision of society; a verbal reflection of dialectical thought; vast analogical metaphors complete in their designs; a virtuosic writing full of the spirit of concreteness, of criticism, polemic and mockery: such are the most prominent features of the style achieved by Marx, who got his start in poetic meditation, who conceived of prose as a work of art, and whose apex consists of a scientific corpus literarily blessed with a prodigious expressive power.

Mastery of prose came to Marx the same way as mastery of verse comes to great poets: all of a sudden and very early, as if it were the manifestation of a linguistic instinct. It is clear that literary and philological study aids this instinct, but this is nothing more than a spur to something that is already there. If Marx progressed and matured in his development of an economic and historical conception of society as he got older, in terms of his literary style he possessed a clearly defined way of expressing himself from a very young age.

In this sense, we can take the final months of 1843 as a starting point. Marx was twenty-five then, and during this time he completed the Introduction to the *Critique of Hegel's Philosophy of Right* (the only part of that work that remains). While it is true that he had already written articles in which it is easy to find many stylistic discoveries (his vibrant articles against the censorship of the press, for example), it is definitely the case that the above-mentioned *Critique* is the first document in which we find a fully developed personal style in Marx. It is not by chance that this is a fragment that 'ended up as an artistic whole', as we have seen occur whenever his materials went to print. In terms of well-rounded 'sentences', this essay is a nursery – one from which many have drawn, to be sure. Many of Marx's phrases that have seen the widest circulation come from it, like the one about how 'to be radical is to grasp things by the root. But for man the root is man himself.'[75] Other less famous, but perhaps more significant, phrases come from it as well: 'Theory is realized in a people only in so far as it is a realization of the people's needs.'[76]

Equally notable is his Feuerbachian critique of religion: '*Man makes religion*, religion does not make man', and the materialist principle that 'man is *the world of man*, state, society. This state and this society produce religion, which is an *inverted consciousness of the world*, because they are an *inverted world*.'[77] And, with respect to the stunted German society of his time: 'These petrified relations must be forced to dance by having their own tune sung to them!' What is the creation of class consciousness if not the idea that 'the people must be taught to be terrified at itself in order to give it courage'?[78] Without a doubt, even though Marx did not yet possess his future scientific wisdom, he was already in control of his expressive wisdom, as this magisterial piece of critical prose demonstrates.

The *1844 Manuscripts* lack this perfection, even though – as we have already shown by citing examples – they are full of stylistically brilliant fragments. But next to these fragments we find others that are insufficiently developed, that are confusing, obscure, and that occasionally deserve the label of 'Heraclitan obscurity' given to them by Peter Demetz. These are mostly philosophical formulations, conveyed in an abstract vocabulary ('human essence', and so on) that Marx himself would mock half a

---

75   Marx, 'Critique of Hegel's *Philosophy of Right*: Introduction', in *Early Writings*, p. 251.
76   Ibid., p. 252.
77   Ibid., p. 244.
78   Ibid., p. 247.

decade later in a passage from the *Communist Manifesto*. It is precisely this philosophical obscurity that has, in our century, served as the point of entry for certain metaphysical Marxologists and even some Christian Marxologists, who, it is clear, could not sneak in through Marx's mature, more scientifically transparent works. It is a shame that those manuscripts could not be polished by their author, and that, on the contrary, they launched the long career of his incomplete works.

An intermediate landmark in this respect is *The German Ideology* (1845–6). It is intermediate because, though it never saw print, it came closer to it than other posthumous manuscripts – in fact, it was on the verge of receiving that final pass. The first part, on Feuerbach, is nevertheless a complete stylistic ensemble, full of masterful ironies directed at philosophers and bourgeois economists. On the subject of philosophical hedonism, Marx tells us that 'the philosophy of enjoyment was never anything but the clever language of certain social circles who had the privilege of enjoyment.'[79] He also refers to the 'forced philosophising imposed . . . by division of labour'[80] that is practised with surgical zeal in German universities. A typical example of the stylistic trademark we have described above (see section two of Chapter 2) is the following argument against Feuerbach: 'As far as Feuerbach is a materialist he does not deal with history, and as far as he considers history he is not a materialist. With him materialism and history diverge completely.'[81] We can say of this text of Marx's (which he co-wrote with Engels) that it integrates for the first time his fully formed expressive style with all the peculiar characteristics derived from his study of economics: it is like watching a squad of philosophical categories parachute down to the firm and crass ground of social reality.

The same can be said of *The Holy Family*, where Marx attacks full on 'the *speculative* terminology in which the concrete is

---

79   Marx and Engels, 'The German Ideology', p. 417.
80   Ibid., p. 312.
81   Ibid., p. 41.

called abstract and the abstract concrete'.[82] On this matter, and against the substantialist tendency to expend great effort in inventing 'categories' and 'entities', he writes:

> How could absolute subjectivity, the *actus purus, 'pure'* Criticism, not see in love its *bête noire*, that Satan incarnate, in love, which first really teaches man to believe in the objective world outside himself, which not only makes man into an object, but even the object into a man! . . . The passion of love is incapable of having an interest in *internal* development because it cannot be construed *a priori*, because its development is a real one which takes place in the world of the senses and between real individuals.[83]

In this work, in particular, we can see a general feature of Marx's style: the ironic smile of one who enjoys fighting philosophers with their own weapons and going beyond them, fighting them from within and without, with a language that is both under control and that exceeds itself. Marx's language in this work displays a great virtuosity, though it is a bit exaggerated to claim, as Mehring does, that it contains 'some of his most marvellous pages'.

The Poverty of Philosophy is perhaps the last text filled with philosophical critique and its corresponding stylistic modes. But we have already spoken of this 1847 work enough in this essay. The *Manifesto of the Communist Party* (1848) and *Wage Labour and Capital* (1849) represent a full integration into socio-economic analysis. The *Manifesto* is an exemplary instance of the *adoption* of literary style as a means to achieve a certain effect on the public: the apocalyptic presentation of events, the description of history as the theatre of dramatically presented class struggle, the terrible predictions, and its overall lyrical aspect, all mark this work as a 'breakwater of eternities', which is

---

82   Marx and Engels, 'The Holy Family', p. 23.
83   Ibid., pp. 21–3.

what Marx and Engels, with good political sense, sought. The lectures on *Wage Labour and Capital* are the first model of an economic analysis that belongs almost completely to the mature Marx, as the references to this work in *Capital* attest. His description of the wage-worker is impeccable, and repeats the pattern of correlations that culminate in a synthesis:

> The worker, who for twelve hours weaves, spins, drills, turns, builds, shovels, breaks stones, carries loads, etc. – does he consider this twelve hours' weaving, spinning, drilling, turning, building, shovelling, stone-breaking as a manifestation of his life, as life? On the contrary, life begins for him where this activity ceases, at table, in the public house, in bed. The twelve hours' labour, on the other hand, has no meaning for him as weaving, spinning, drilling, etc., but as *earnings*, which bring him to the table, to the public house, into bed. If the silkworm were to spin in order to continue its existence as a caterpillar, it would be a complete wage-worker. [Wenn der Seidenwurm spänne, um seine Existenz als Raupe zu fristen, so wäre er ein vollständiger Lohnarbeiter.][84]

We can clearly see in this fragment the loving stylistic care of someone who presents something as finished, and the clarity of someone who has abandoned certain arduous philosophemes in order to explain the problem of alienation represented by the wage and the 'making unreal' of the worker.

Between 1850 and 1852, Marx writes *The Class Struggles in France* and *The Eighteenth Brumaire of Louis Bonaparte*, two models of political history that inspired hate and did nothing more than increase the poverty of the Marx family: 'For the past 8–10 days I have been feeding the family solely on bread and potatoes, but whether I shall be able to get hold of any today is

---

84   Karl Marx, 'Wage Labour and Capital', in *Karl Marx and Friedrich Engels Collected Works*, Vol. 9, Lawrence and Wishart, 2010, p. 203.

doubtful',[85] he wrote to Engels on 8 September 1852. The incisive, implacable style of a writer who refused to be cowed, even by his own poverty, had its effect.

From then until the time of the *Grundrisse*, Marx was a victim of journalism. Hundreds of articles that contributed little to his scientific production (with isolated exceptions such as his magnificent article on 'The British Rule in India', where he affirms that by destroying the economic base of the communities in Hindustan, England 'was the unconscious tool of history' and played a revolutionary social role); poverty and more poverty; creditors, and, above all, his need to employ his labour-power as a journalistic commodity: an ironic situation of alienation that was wholly conscious and all the more painful for it.

We have already offered our stylistic assessment of the *Grundrisse* and the *Critique of Political Economy* (see the second section of Chapter 2). Our judgement can be repeated almost verbatim in the case of both *Capital* and that appendix to it that has acquired a life of its own, much like the tail-end of an annelid that has been lopped off: *Theorien über den Mehrwert*, which was translated into Spanish by W. Roces (based on Kautsky's incomplete edition) as *The Critical History of Surplus Value*, for some reason, though it should perhaps have been called simply *Theories of Surplus Value* or, to be more explicit, *The Critical History of Bourgeois Economics*. As we know, *Capital* was meant to encompass Marx's entire theoretical system as a kind of river-work or *roman-fleuve*. But, out of all that effortful research and thinking, only one volume (Volume 1) was ever 'completed and sent to the printer'; this, without a doubt, explains the manifest superiority of Volume 1 over Volumes 2 and 3, at least in terms of literary quality. Given that they were prepared for publication by Engels, Volumes 2 and 3 represent an intermediate point, however: even though Engels polished and edited them, he never let his own style fly above that of Marx's manuscript, which gives a *general* air of stylistic

---

85   'Marx to Engels', in *Karl Marx and Friedrich Engels Collected Works*, Vol. 39, Lawrence and Wishart, 2010, p. 181.

imprecision and opacity to these two volumes. Nevertheless, they are full of definitive fragments that Marx would doubtlessly have left intact. Volume 3, for example, contains his remarkable treatment of interest-bearing capital (*zinstragende Kapital*), something that might sound like the most tedious possible topic, but that, in Marx's hands, becomes 'the most fetish-like form [of capital]', the form in which money, the supreme fetish, *appears* to reproduce itself by an act of transubstantiation (represented in the formula M-M') without the intervention of human labour. This fetish in fact hides an absolute concentration of dead or objectified labour that rises up, through the magic of banking and finance, as an all-encompassing power at the heart of society that is set against the producers, the owners of living labour. Marx successively refers to this form of capital as *die reine Fetischform* (the pure form of the fetish), *die dinglichste Form* (the most thing-like form), the *vollständigste Fetisch* (the most perfect fetish), the *fetischartigste Form* (the most fetishistic form) or, simply, *Fetischismus*. And so, the theory of fetishism, developed in Volume 1, reaches in Volume 3, with regards to the 'trinity formula', a highly developed literary expression, one also found in *Theories of Surplus Value* (that is, Volume 4). It has to be this way because, as he writes in Volume 3:

> Capital–profit (or better still capital–interest), land–ground rent, labour–wages, this economic trinity (*ökonomisch Trinität*) as the connection between the components of value and wealth in general and its sources, completes the mystification of the capitalist mode of production, the reification (*Verdinglichung*) of social relations, and the immediate coalescence of the material relations of production with their historical and social specificity: the bewitched, distorted and upside-down world haunted by Monsieur le Capital and Madame la Terre who are at the same time social characters and mere things. It is the great merit of classical economics [of which Marx was the crown jewel – L.S.] to have dissolved this false appearance and deception, this autonomization and ossification of the different social elements of wealth vis-à-vis one another, this

personification of things and reification of the relations of production, this religion of everyday life ... [!!!][86]

This characterization of the monetary and commercial economy as a *religion of everyday life* (*diese Religion des Alltagslebens*) represents the culmination and perfection of the great metaphor of religion (also stylistically present here in the holy 'trinity formula') which we have analysed above (see the third part of Chapter 2).

The most stylistically successful parts of *Theories of Surplus Value* treat precisely these topics. The architecture of this unfinished work is simpler and more linear than that of Marx's other works: it proceeds historically and analyses one economist after another. It begins by citing sources, it presents fragments for study, and then it engages in a critique that is almost always devastating but remains also fair, especially when it comes to recognizing the merits of classical economics, without which Marx would never have arrived at his theories of labour-power and surplus-value. This work includes many 'dialectical' sentences of the kind we examined in the second part of Chapter 2. Compare, for example, the sentences of the *1844 Manuscripts* we have already analysed (in which we highlighted the play of opposites) with these from *Theories of Surplus Value: Part 3*: 'In this contradiction, political economy merely expressed the essence of capitalist production or, if you like, of wage labour, of *labour alienated from itself,*

which stands confronted by the wealth it has created	as alien wealth
by its own productive power	as the productive power *of its product*
by its enrichment	as its own impoverishment
by its social power	as the power of society.'[87]

---

86   Karl Marx, *Capital, Volume 3*, trans. David Fernbach, Penguin, 1991, pp. 968–9.

87   Karl Marx, *Theories of Surplus Value: Part 3*, Lawrence and

From 1867, when he published Volume 1 of *Capital*, until his death in 1883, Marx's labour-power gradually declined. The standout texts of this period include his writings on Russia (a country he studied with unusual intensity, going so far as to learn the Russian language) and his *Critique of the Gotha Programme* of 1875, in which he develops, as he did years before in the *Grundrisse*, a grand prospective vision of communist society which retains its viability to this day and which has not, whatever anyone says, been invalidated by the *transition* to socialism of several societies, but which has, on the contrary, been profoundly affirmed by the appearance in the most highly developed industrial nations of a series of structural preconditions that can serve as the basis of a future socialist society. It is there that Marx writes his great *scientific* utopia:

> In a more advanced phase of communist society, when the enslaving subjugation of individuals to the division of labour, and thereby the antithesis between intellectual and physical labour, have disappeared; when labour is no longer just a means of keeping alive but has itself become a vital need; when the all-around development of individuals has also increased their productive powers and all the springs of cooperative wealth flow more abundantly – only then can society wholly cross the narrow horizon of bourgeois right and inscribe on its banners: 'From each according to his abilities, to each according to his needs!'[88]

Wishart, 1971, p. 259. 'In diesem Widerspruch sprach die politische Ökonomie bloß das Wesen der kapitalistischen Produktion aus oder, wenn man will, der Lohnarbeit aus; der sich selbst *entfremdeten Arbeit*, der der von ihr geschaffene Reichtum als fremder Reichtum, ihre eigne Produktivkraft als Produktivkraft ihres Produkts, ihre Bereicherung als Selbstverarmung, ihre gesellschaftliche Macht als Macht der Gesellschaft über sie gegenübertritt.' Karl Marx, *Theorien über Mehrwert, Marx-Engels Werke*, Vol. 23.3, Dietz Verlag, pp. 254–5.

88   Karl Marx, 'Critique of the Gotha Program', in *The Political Writings*, Verso, 2019, p. 1031.

Such was Marx's stylistic parabola: the ends ultimately meet. Do not the same ideas – and nearly the same words – about the conditions for the universal overcoming of alienation appear in the *1844 Manuscripts* and in this late text?

Marx is surprised by death on 14 March 1883. As Engels tells Sorge, doctors could have prolonged his life for a few years, but his would have been a vegetative existence, and how could Marx have tolerated such a life, given how much work he had left to finish and how much his desire to do so would have tortured him? It would have been 'more bitter than the gentle death which overtook him'. 'In the space of two minutes he had passed away painlessly and peacefully.'[89]

There is a text of Marx's that is little known despite its beauty and perspicacity, and that contains all the characteristics of his style that we have identified. It is a fragment of a speech he gave on the occasion of the fourth anniversary of the *People's Paper* on 14 April 1856:

> In our days, everything seems pregnant with its contrary. Machinery, gifted with the wonderful power of shortening and fructifying human labour, we behold starving and over-working it. The new-fangled sources of wealth, by some strange weird spell, are turned into sources of want. The victories of art seem bought by the loss of character. At the same pace that mankind masters nature, man seems to become enslaved to other men or to his own infamy. Even the pure light of science seems unable to shine but on the dark background of ignorance. All our invention and progress seem to result in endowing material forces with intellectual life, and in stultifying human life into a material force. This antagonism between modern industry and science on the one hand, modern misery and dissolution on the other hand; this

---

89   'Engels to Friedrich Adolph Sorge, 15 March 1883', in *Karl Marx and Friedrich Engels Collected Works*, Vol. 46, Lawrence and Wishart, 2010, p. 462.

antagonism between the productive powers and the social relations of our epoch is a fact, palpable, overwhelming, and not to be controverted. Some parties may wail over it; others may wish to get rid of modern arts, in order to get rid of modern conflicts. Or they may imagine that so signal a progress in industry wants to be completed by as signal a regress in politics. On our part, we do not mistake the shape of the shrewd spirit that continues to mark all these contradictions. We know that to work well the new-fangled forces of society, they only want to be mastered by new-fangled men – and such are the working men. They are as much the invention of modern time as machinery itself. In the signs that bewilder the middle class, the aristocracy and the poor prophets of regression, we do recognise our brave friend, Robin Goodfellow, the old mole that can work in the earth so fast, that worthy pioneer – the Revolution [. . .] To revenge the misdeeds of the ruling class, there existed in the Middle Ages, in Germany, a secret tribunal, called the 'Vehmgericht'. If a red cross was seen marked on a house, people knew that its owner was doomed by the 'Vehm'. All the houses of Europe are now marked with the mysterious red cross. History is the judge – its executioner, the proletarian.[90]

---

90   Karl Marx, 'Speech at the Anniversary of *The People's Paper*', in *Karl Marx and Friedrich Engels Collected Works*, Vol. 14, Lawrence and Wishart, 2010, pp. 655–66.

Epilogue on Irony and Alienation

In *The Class Struggles in France* (1850), Marx writes in golden letters: 'The mortgage the peasant has on heavenly possessions guarantees the mortgage the bourgeois has on peasant possessions.'[1]

This brief sentence, whose conceptual and stylistic brilliance jumps out – or, to use the German phrase Marx favoured, 'screams in your face': *ins Gesicht schreien* – encompasses all of the stylistic characteristics I have highlighted in this study.

Architectonically speaking, the sentence is perfect. It also participates in what we have called the 'dialectic of expression', which is also an 'expression of the dialectic'. It features a combination common in Marx: irony mixed with indignation. How many have tried to imitate Marx's style, only to copy the indignation while forgetting the irony! To be able to imitate Marx's style gracefully, one would need to recall that the entire machinery of his indignation is mounted on the serrated gear of his irony.

The conceptual mode of Marx's irony is always determined by that infinite capacity he possessed for seeing all social phenomena *upside down* – for seeing their inverse, where economists, philosophers and politicians only see their semblance, their

---

1   Marx, 'The Class Struggles in France: 1848–50', in *The Political Writings*, p. 420. 'Die Hypotheke, welche der Bauer auf die himmlischen Güter besitzt, garantiert die Hypotheke, welche der Bourgeois auf die Bauerngüter besitzt.' Karl Marx and Friedrich Engels, *Ausgewählte Schriften*, Vol. 1, Dietz Verlag, 1958, p. 168.

obverse. And the perceptual or stylistic mode for transmitting that 'cunning of reason' comes from his no-less-infinite capacity for constructing statements and sentences with ascending phases that ironically present the obverse, the semblance of things ('the mortgage the peasant has on heavenly possessions'), and descending phases that contain their inverse, that is, the hidden structure of phenomena ('guarantees the mortgage the bourgeois has on peasant possessions').

Throughout this book, I have sought to demonstrate that these stylistic modes are not coincidences, clever brainstorms, or the simple ornaments with which a scientist might dress up his prose in order to make it more accessible. Instead, and on the contrary, they form a harmonious whole with the conceptual system that they, as stylistic modes, convey. For instance, the feature we have just noted is the stylistic formula which gives definitive expression to a central problem of Marx's thought. That irony that first describes the happy appearance of social relations only to then denounce their miserable true structure; that immense indictment of classical and vulgar economics, a discipline which limits itself to a description of the apparent functions of capital and so obscures its antagonistic relationship to labour – these are nothing more than the concrete and special application of Marx's general conception of history. If Marx is a materialist, it is because he always sought to discover, by going beyond or beneath the ideological appearance of historical events (state, law, religion, morality, metaphysics), their underlying material structures. This is why his stylistic ironies always play a key role: that of denunciation, of the illumination of reality. 'The whole of historical development consists, according to the ideologist, in the theoretical abstractions of that development which have taken shape in the "heads" of all "the philosophers and theologians of the age"', he tells us in *The German Ideology*.[2] In other words, the irony

---

2   Marx and Engels, 'The German Ideology', in *Karl Marx and Friedrich Engels Collected Works*, Vol. 5, Lawrence and Wishart, 2010, p. 532.

which is always at play in Marx is not a mere detail but one of the keys to understanding his conception of history. It is often said that Marx is ironic and derisive simply because those were features of his psychological makeup. Judging by the testimonies of Mehring and others and by his correspondence, which is as valuable in its field as Flaubert's is in his, they certainly were. Marx was fearsome and aggressive. Nevertheless, we would commit a great error in perspective if we were to reduce all of this to a psychological or 'temperamental' trait. It is also a question of theoretical temperament: irony, mockery and *critique* in general – how many of Marx's works begin with the word 'critique'? – were all integral parts of his general theory of society and history. Societies throughout history present themselves as politico-legal 'results', and the ideologue, good intellectual ostrich that he is, after swallowing a mouthful of the real material causes of events, limits himself to superficially declaring that societies are their 'results' and in so doing elevates these results to the status of premises. Thus, effects appear as causes, and ideology appears to be the true engine of history.

Engels used to say that what characterized ideology, in the *strict* sense of the term, was that it treats thoughts, systems and conceptual worlds (*Gedankenwelt*) as independent worlds, objects and autonomous 'essences' (*selbständigen Wesenheiten*), and in so doing loses sight of reality. Engels's contribution to the theory of ideology was as great as Marx's. But it is the latter who gives us the best material that we might take as 'empirical' for the study of ideology in its specific manifestations. Volume 3 of *Capital*, for instance, is filled with observations on the Appearance/ Structure dyad, that is, on those social appearances (the state, the legal regime, and so on) that dazzle the economists and make them forget the real foundations upon which these appearances rest. Political economy is ghostly: it sees nothing but spectres, ghostly apparitions, fantasies, the fetishes in which society clothes itself and that constitute, strictly speaking, its ideology. It can only see what is present to its naked eye, and in this way acts more or less like a bacteriologist who studies bacteria without the aid of a microscope. In the field of social science, it is not a question of handling a microscope but of handling *abstraction*. Marx was so conscious of this that it was the first thing he noted in the Preface to the first edition of *Capital*:

> I have popularized the passages concerning the substance of value and the magnitude of value as much as possible. The value-form, whose fully developed shape is the money-form, is very simple and slight in content. Nevertheless, the human mind has sought in vain for more than 2,000 years to get to the bottom of it, while on the other hand there has been at least an approximation to a successful analysis of forms which are much richer in content and more complex. Why? Because the complete body is easier to study than its cells. Moreover, in the analysis of economic forms neither microscopes nor chemical reagents are of assistance. The power of abstraction must replace both. But for bourgeois society, the commodity-form of the product of labour, or the value-form of the commodity, is the economic cell-form.[3]

The ideologue considers society and sees it as a 'complete body': he sees a state, a legal regime, a regime of private property that is enshrined in the law and made eternal, he sees 'iron laws', he sees bourgeois legal 'equality', and so on; but he does not see the economic power behind the state, the economic interests behind the legal regime, the expropriation of some by others behind the laws of private property, the iron of the economic yoke behind the iron laws, the profound social inequality behind the legal equality.

It is therefore necessary to engage in a radical critique of ideology. A critique which in Marx is stylistically paired with *irony*. No critique is as devastating as that which goes from irony to denunciation and from denunciation to irony. In

---

3   Marx, *Capital, Volume 1*, pp. 89–90.

Marx's writing, and, in particular, in those works which he finished and published, this feature acquires an infinite level of nuance.

It goes from rendering certain details ironic to rendering the entire capital system ironic, all while poking brutal fun at the system's apologists. An example of the ironic detail is the fragment from the *Critique of Political Economy* quoted in the Introduction to the present study: 'one volume of Propertius and eight ounces of snuff may have the same exchange-value, despite the dissimilar use-values of snuff and elegies'. Why reach for the elegist Propertius in order to compare him to eight ounces of snuff? The reason for this choice is genuinely stylistic. How can one characterize in a single sentence an entire economic system based on exchange-value, on the 'value' of the commodity form, a system in which the use-values of goods are of secondary importance? The best way would appear to be to point out ironically that exchange-value has a levelling power so overwhelming that anything, no matter how elevated or illustrious it might be, is reduced to the same *value* as anything else, no matter how pedestrian the latter is, as long as the two have equal magnitudes. In other words: we have an economic system based on the category of *quantity*, that possesses an all-encompassing power over the *quality* of not only things but people as well. And so, while the eight ounces of snuff admit comparison to the volume of Propertius, what is truly grave is that *human labour-power* can be made equivalent. After all, one of Marx's great economic discoveries involved seeing that in capitalism *labour-power* possesses a specific *use-value* capable of sustaining an *exchange-value*, that is, labour-power is a *commodity* that is sold in the labour market for a wage and which possesses the characteristic that most fascinates the owner of capital; namely, it is a commodity capable of producing other commodities, a machine fuelled by wages rather than gas or coal, specifically by the minimum wage necessary for preserving its status as a labour-power. That this commodity thinks, suffers, laughs, cries and loves – these are no more than insignificant additions. As Marx says in *Capital*, the golden gates of the capitalist system bear a sign that reads: *No admittance except on business.*[4]

The first volume of *Capital* – which is, from the point of view of scientific prose, one of the most perfect works ever written, possessed of an expressive magnetism comparable to that of Plato's *Phaedrus* – contains a chapter on the division of labour (I, chapter 12) in which Marx takes the stylistic phenomenon we have been discussing as far as it can go. To speak of the division of labour is, for Marx, to speak of the primordial factor – both synchronically and diachronically speaking – of *alienation*. With time, the division of labour, which began – as *The German Ideology* tells us – with the division between physical and intellectual labour and the consolidation of a dominant administrative-religious social sector, becomes the most distant and radical factor of human alienation. It is only later that the other two decisive factors of alienation arise: private property and commodity production, which, along with the division of labour, constitute, now more than ever, the matrix of variables that explain alienation as a *historical, and therefore superable,* phenomenon – conquerable through the overcoming of the material factors in question. And even though some of these factors preceded others in time, a synchronic vision of contemporary capitalist society must consider them as a set of interlocking, mutually inter-dependent variables. In this analytical vision, what was historically a 'cause' can appear as an 'effect': given that private property, for example, is a historical cause of alienation, it can, in its present concrete forms, be derived through analysis (*durch Analyse*, Marx specifically says) from alienation, and can thus appear as an 'effect' of alienation. It is worth mention-ing, in passing, that this allows us to resolve an apparent contradiction that some have found in the *1844 Manuscripts*, specifically in a passage in which private property is treated as an 'effect', rather than as a 'cause', of alienation. Until now, no

---

4   Marx, *Capital, Volume 1*, p. 280.

one has noticed that Marx speaks quite concretely about the possibility of deriving private property from alienation, but only *durch Analyse*. This is because the *logical precedence* of the concept of alienation with regards to private property is one thing, and the *real, historical precedence* of private property with respect to alienation quite another (at least insofar as we currently understand the latter after 7,000 years of history – if we think back to the most primitive form of alienation, that caused by the division of labour back when property was communal and collective, we can conceive of private property as a historical 'effect' of that alienation that had previously arisen with the division of labour).

Returning to our main subject, in the passage from *Capital* we have alluded to above and which is focused on the division of labour, we find Marx's most stylistically brilliant description of alienation in the realm of production or, as he liked to say, 'the *hidden* abode of production'. Let us read one of its most characteristic fragments:

> In manufacture, as well as in simple co-operation, the collective working organism is a form of existence of capital. The social mechanism of production, which is made up of numerous individual specialized workers, belongs to the capitalist. Hence the productive power which results from the combination of various kinds of labour appears as the productive power of capital. Manufacture proper not only subjects the previously independent worker to the discipline and command of capital, but creates in addition a hierarchical structure amongst the workers themselves [Is this the origin of the contemporary labour bureaucracy? – L.S.]. While simple co-operation leaves the mode of the individual's labour for the most part unchanged, manufacture thoroughly revolutionizes it, and seizes labour-power by its roots. It converts the worker into a crippled monstrosity by furthering his particular skill as in a forcing-house, through the suppression of a whole world of productive drives and inclinations, just as in

the states of La Plata they butcher a whole beast for the sake of his hide or his tallow. Not only is the specialized work distributed among the different individuals, but the individual himself is divided up, and transformed into the automatic motor of a detail operation, thus realizing the absurd fable of Menenius Agrippa, which presents man as a mere fragment of his own body . . . As the chosen people bore in their features the sign that they were the property of Jehovah, so the division of labour brands the manufacturing worker as the property of capital.[5]

Passages that combine such scientific precision with such literary precision are not at all common in scientific literature. The quoted passage is emblematic of a science like Marx's that understands itself as a form of denunciation. For this science, empirical objectivity is no obstacle to ethico-political judgement. This is why this science is so profoundly irritating to all those scientists who serve capital. They try in vain to tar *Capital* as 'ideological' when *Capital* itself is precisely the greatest critique of ideology ever mounted! Ideological science is, on the contrary, mobilized to serve capital and submissive to its dictates and needs. Immediately after the above-quoted passage, Marx puts this with exemplary clarity: 'This process of separation starts in simple co-operation, where the capitalist represents to the individual workers the unity and the will of the whole body of social labour. It is developed in manufacture, which mutilates the worker, turning him into a fragment of himself. It is completed in large-scale industry, which makes science a potentiality for production which is distinct from labour and presses it into the service of capital.'

And what can be said of science can be said of culture as a whole. In this same passage, Marx cites a very significant sentence by W. Thompson:

---

5   Marx, *Capital, Volume 1*, pp. 481–2.

'The man of knowledge and the productive labourer come to be widely divided from each other, and knowledge, instead of remaining the handmaid of labour in the hand of the labourer to increase his productive powers ... has almost everywhere arrayed itself against labour.' 'Knowledge' becomes 'an instrument, capable of being detached from labour and opposed to it.'[6]

Why, then, does this hypostasis or alienation of science from culture occur with respect to the producers? Marx allows us to glimpse – and it is a shame that he does not expand upon this point – the true reason behind this phenomenon when he writes:

The colonial system and the extension of the world market, both of which form part of the general conditions for the existence of the manufacturing period, furnish us with rich materials for displaying the division of labour in society. *This is not the place, however, for us to show how division of labour seizes upon, not only the economic, but every other sphere of society*, and everywhere lays the foundation for that specialization, that *development in a man of one single faculty at the expense of all others*, which already caused Adam Ferguson, the master of Adam Smith, to exclaim: 'We make a nation of Helots, and have no free citizens.'[7]

Here, then, is the profound reason behind the general alienation that affects the capitalist system in every one of its social spheres in the twentieth century, a hundred years after *Capital* was written. What wouldn't Marx say about the specialization of man in a world dominated by the major corporations of monopoly capital in which the division of labour has reached an astounding extreme? He would see the confirmation of the

6   Marx, *Capital, Volume 1*, pp. 482–3, note 44.
7   Ibid., p. 474 (italics mine – L.S.).

crass truth of his scientific predictions. Marx was, after all, a *predictive* scientist, not the 'prophet' that he has been zealously, religiously portrayed as.

Now, as I have already implied in various parts of this essay, Marx's own work is the best demonstration he could have left us of how the overcoming of alienation begins with the overcoming of the present form of the division of labour. There are no traces of 'the division of labour' within it: Proteus-like, Marx engaged in all manner of study and incorporated all kinds of ancient and modern materials in his research; he blended diverse disciplines in the enormous river of a comprehensive social science, which is in itself the best possible argument against the estrangement brought about by 'specialization'; he denounced political economy as an ideological alienation that separates out economic facts from the totality of social facts; on top of that, he coupled his theories with practical political struggle, suffering exile, hunger, poverty and the deaths of his children, all while cementing the foundations of proletarian internationalism. And within this brilliantly harmonious panorama, Marx always attempted to imbue his works with a dazzling literary power – after all, as well as being a sociologist, economist, historian, linguist and so on, he was also a great writer in the greatest neo-Latin literary tradition.

In his splendid work *European Literature and the Latin Middle Ages*, the romanticist Ernst Robert Curtius presents an incisive catalogue of the metaphorical forms that could be considered genuinely neo-Latin: the metaphor of the *Theatrum mundi*, nautical metaphors, metaphors of the body, metaphors of the person and so on. All of these metaphors are scattered throughout Marx's writings, some of them in the form of classical allusions, others present in his practice of creating new metaphors based on models laid down by the rhetorics of the Greco-Latin and medieval worlds.

But the best of all the metaphors discovered by Marx is gigantic: it is *capitalist society taken as a whole.* The Greek word 'metaphor' means *translatio* or to transfer from one meaning to another. In capitalist society we find a strange and all-encompassing transfer from the real meaning of human life towards a distorted meaning. The capitalist metaphor is *alienation*. In the Middle Ages, *alienatio* meant 'transference' or movement from one meaning to another: from the proper meaning of a word to an improper meaning. This 'impropriety' can end up being positive and beautiful, as when we make literary metaphors and speak, for example, of the Platonic 'sun of ideas' or of the 'eyes of the soul'; but it can also be negative, as when we make a word mean something it truly does not and in so doing produce confusion or ambiguity. The same thing occurs with capitalist *alienation*, which is nothing but a monstrous metaphor. In capitalist society, the meaning of use-value – the meaning of quality – is expropriated from itself and substituted by the meaning of exchange-value, of *quantity*. It is no surprise that Marx translated the English word *expropriation* as *Entäusserung*, which is the word we usually translate as *alienation*. In this society, it is generally believed that it is ideology that holds up the social edifice, and not that ideology rests on the foundation constituted by the socioeconomic structure of society. In this society, the division of labour is the division of the worker; private property is fed by public expropriation; the production of the market is not driven by human needs but instead by the needs of the market itself – an aberrant social tautology; culture and science do not aid human flourishing, but rather drive the compartmentalization of man, if not war; the prodigious development of productive forces ceaselessly generates tremendous wealth that, nevertheless, falls into a regime of private appropriation; and, in the end, concrete man has been supplanted by abstract man, who is, in Marx's theory, the *social* producer of wealth.

Is this whole transference of meanings not a gigantic metaphor, a living metaphor? Is the alienation of man not a spectral metaphor that makes us live in an inverted world, where everything is 'pregnant with its opposite', as Marx claimed?

This is why the ultimate stylistic achievement of this exceptional man was to present the capitalist world as standing on its own feet, something he could only accomplish after discovering its metaphorical character, its alienated structure.